***

ROCK THE BOAT

Hilary Harrison

contributions by

Thomas Harrison & Celeste Harrison

***

For Robin,

with gratitude

***

Contents

Foreword

Sixteen years ago, my wife and I attended Hilary and Thomas's wedding on their lovely barge Golden Mean, on a fine stretch of the upper Thames. Never in our wildest dreams did we envisage the barge as a permanent home, believing it to be just a passing whim; totally impractical as a long term home.

How wrong could we be! One only has to meet their teenage children; two of the nicest most balanced youngsters, to see first-hand witness of the astonishing success Hilary and Thomas have made of their lives in the very unusual setting of a steel barge.

Their story really is an inspiration to all setting out as a newly married couple, proving that future happiness need not depend on the conventional view that four walls, three bedrooms and a garden are essential!

Well told in this small book, the author holds the reader's interest to the end, with plenty of illustrations on overcoming the many obstacles that confronted them.

Robin Combe, June 2021

Introduction

An eight-year old girl leaned forward from the back seat and hugged the broad frame of the driver, before scrambling out with her school bag and disappearing from view through the open gate in the low flint boundary wall that secured the sloping playground. Following a well-trodden path, her father pulled into the church car park and circled the car back towards the direction from whence they came.

As a younger man Philip Gardner served in World War Two as a spitfire pilot, followed by some years running an advertising partnership in London. Now in his late fifties he had swopped the thrill of the aircraft carrier landing for a more sedate life as watercolour painter, spending his days in blissful solitude in his studio at the bottom of the garden of his flint cottage in North Norfolk. Reluctant to leave his newly adopted home county, his good friend Robin (who dropped in to visit him in his studio most days) joked that he was in a rut. 'A comfortable rut' he would reply, with a puff of pipe smoke, feeling entirely justified.

Philip was tall and sturdily built, with long legs which caused him considerate discomfort on longer journeys. In truth he avoided long journeys if at all possible. However, on occasions such as the school drop-off, his stature was a blessing. His knees were perfectly positioned to take control of the steering wheel. A stunt which enabled him to wave goodbye with both hands to his only daughter, who duly waited in position, now inside the flint wall. In later years the wall would be flanked by a high metal fence and it would no longer be thought safe (nor indeed necessary) for boys to dash out through the gate to retrieve an errant football off the road during boisterous break-times. This was a ritual the girl and her father performed every morning - prior to the necessary separation that their respective purposes of education and watercolour painting entailed.

Content that Hilary had had an appropriate send-off, Philip drove down the steep high street flanked by flint cottages and hollyhocks. He was not alone in the car. His beloved smooth coated border collie Moss sat erect in the boot, barely noticing the daughter's wave, as she knew that the morning walk along Blakeney 'carnser' was only a matter of minutes away. First though, she had to patiently wait a little longer, whilst her master had his daily interchange with The Sausage Provider. Sydney Loose the butcher, occupied a small blue and white fronted shop near the bottom of Blakeney High Street. Nowadays Sydney's simple and essential shop hosts an upmarket deli, supplying tourists with posh picnic fodder.

Moss endured the delay in her walk beginning, due to Philip's daily conversation with Sydney, as she knew that there was a good chance she might later get to share a morsel of whatever was in the package that always accompanied him when he returned. Something wrapped in greaseproof paper and encased in a stripey blue and white plastic bag, to match the shop front. In her opinion the wrapping barely masked the smell of delicious fat homemade sausages or proper thick back bacon that it contained. Had she not the greatest respect for her master, Moss could easily have consumed the package on the way home whilst Philip was distracted lighting his pipe for the millionth time. She had to admit she'd thought about it. But as appealing as that might be in the moment, the idea of the disappointment that Philip would undoubtedly bestow on her, albeit wordless, meant that displeasing her adored owner was anathema to Moss. One of those loyal dogs that really only likes one person, Moss spent every waking moment at his side – and most of these in his studio at the bottom of the garden. A few years later, it would become necessary to transfer her allegiance to Hilary, but for now Philip was the object of her desire.

Almost more attractive was the anticipation of the moment, perhaps later that day or the next morning, where Philip would cut the rind from the bacon, and then, with a subtle flick of the scissors - that appeared to the untrained eye almost accidental - it would be tossed casually, yet intentionally she knew, in her direction. She salivated at the prospect.

Moss brought her attention back to the present as they were now about to enjoy the best hour of the day. Philip and Moss left the car and headed, as they always did, towards the rickety wooden bridge that spanned the first muddy dyke. Hilary, who would by now be singing hymns in assembly, once got stuck here in this very dyke and had to be dis-attached from her wellies in the process. Philip's granddaughter would suffer the same misfortune, some forty years later.

Mud is rather a feature of Blakeney. If you've had the good fortune to walk there, perhaps with a canine friend or as a youngster experiencing the delights of making a mud slide down from the salt marsh into the creek at low tide, you will know that a certain smell lingers on your journey home. It lingers for days, maybe weeks; on your boots, in your fingernails, on the upholstery of your car and on the hair of your dog. A smell that reminds you of that bleak and windswept bit of salt marsh that curves out towards Blakeney Point where the Grey and Common seals pack the Bishop, Bean and Temple seal boats year after year, where a plethora of boats both new and old bob on their moorings in the outer harbour, affectionately known as 'the pit'. A smell that is as evocative as the call of an oystercatcher or the tinkle of halyards on the masts of dinghies resting on the hard at the end of the carpark, just before the little bridge takes you closer to where the sand dunes meet the sky in the distance. Where the Watch House makes its iconic presence in many a painting. A smell that brings you home, even when you've been gone for decades.

Moss and Philip followed the narrow path that is flanked with spikey heather and rocks, where sand and mud converge with broken shells and pebbles. At the right time of year samphire grows in this unique habitat which spends half of its time submerged in salty water. They look ahead to the horizon, the North Sea can't be seen from here but it's not far away, behind the sand dunes and the shingle bank a couple of miles ahead of them, beyond a maze of creeks, some leading somewhere, others leading nowhere.

If you have a smallish boat, you can turn right and follow a creek to Cley and have breakfast at the windmill. Another local icon. Turn left for the pit, the point and the seals. If you've set off from Morston as the seal boats do nowadays, you may sail back to Blakeney and have breakfast on the quay served by a continuation of caravans that for years have prime location on the carpark (above the high tide mark) for this very purpose. Beyond the outer harbour and the seals lies 'the bar' - the place where the open ocean meets the harbour, that infamous sandbank only to be crossed by experienced sea dogs. Things can go wrong very quickly at sea.

Philip and Moss walk as far as they can walk without crossing any creeks, which although just knee high at low water will be impassable in a few hours when the tide comes in. Moss smells the smells only dogs can fully appreciate and Philip re-lights his pipe and looks out towards the sea. Since Hilary started at primary school they haven't been out on the boat so often, although he thinks about it most days, especially on their morning walks. 'Partridge II', (named after Philip's wife who was affectionately nicknamed Partridge by one of his friends) is a converted crab boat. A sturdy clinker built hull some 20 feet long, enclosed at the front by a small cabin, a fixed table that turns into a bed - a gas hob for tea making and probably a few other important nautical knick-knacks that I can't remember. 'Partridge II' is moored at Blakeney on the quay near The Red House. When Philip and Partridge were weekend visitors from London to their North Norfolk cottage they used to head out to the pit every weekend, with bacon butties cut from thick slices of white bread, oozing with butter and mustard and of course Sydney's bacon; still slightly warm, wrapped in foil.

Dropping an anchor, they would enjoy the breakfast and perhaps a wade to the point. Just as fish and chips only really taste best on the beach wrapped in paper, so bacon butties are in their prime when eaten at Blakeney, slightly warm, after an early start to catch the beginning of the tide giving you maximum time out on the water. There would be other boaters out of course, but the harbour is big enough for nobody to feel jostled and the atmosphere convivial - whilst at the same time feeling like the beauty of the place was created just for you. This was just the sort of thing that they had moved up from London permanently for, a few years before Hilary had arrived. They would go out on the early tide this weekend, he told Moss, who licked her lips with anticipation of the bacon rind that morning would bring.

Even the most seasoned of sailors is upstaged sooner or later by the tides. Blakeney pit dries out almost fully at low water, and the creek between the mainland and the point - which is really a long peninsula starting down the coast at Cley and running parallel to the shore as far as Stiffkey, but still ever changing shape due to coastal erosion.   Accessible at low tide from Morston or Blakeney only to those prepared for a long walk and a wade through the creek at thigh height. Philip recalled the time that the family had, by error of judgement on his part, found themselves stranded in the pit on 'Partridge II', unable to navigate back to the quay due to the fast receding waters. He remembered wading through the thick, oily Blakeney mud to get back to the car on the quay, carrying Hilary aged about 4, on his broad shoulders. Her nervous 'I'm not used to this' was deflating to his ego, as he struggled to stay vertical when every step threatened to send them both sprawling.   But explaining their predicament to Hilary was nothing compared to the embarrassment of having to leave the boat publicly high and dry on the sand, to await a higher tide to effect a successful return voyage. Even The Albatross, a huge Dutch barge home to the famous pancake restaurant on Wells quay, with her seasoned Dutch captain, spent some six conspicuous months stuck on the sand somewhere outside of Wells harbour, waiting for a higher tide and enduring the knowing exchanges from smug locals.

Perhaps this is one of the attractions of boats - at least for the more adventurous - things can go wrong at any moment. There is always a tension, variables that can't be controlled; the tide, the weather, dodgy equipment, other boats and boaters. And yet there is nothing more intoxicating than being out on the water, be it calm or choppy, alone or with friends, at the mercy of the elements and symbiotic with the wildlife. If it's a sailing boat then a favourable wind fills your sails to whip you across the open expanse of salty sea waving to seal heads that appear and disappear at random, watching you like puppies with their knowing and doleful eyes. Canoers, fishermen, sailors, river day trippers, lifeboat men - people of all ages and stages of life - leave the daily grind behind on the shore and, for as long as it lasts: embrace a new freedom on the water, timelessness, something close to a mystical experience in which you are truly in the moment, at one with your Creator and all of creation.

Prologue

Forty something years after declaring 'I'm not used to this' from my father's shoulders as he was slip sliding in the Blakeney mud, I'm beginning to 'get used to' the boating life. I can only speculate on what my father would have thought of his only daughter moving onto a sailing barge on the River Thames with her boyfriend in her late twenties, and still living aboard eighteen years later, with her now-husband and two teenage children. There are many things to speculate when you have lost a parent. Children intrinsically want their parents to be proud of them and anyone who's lost a parent will know that this instinct doesn't wane after the parent has died.

I'm fortunate to have a godfather in the wings, someone who my father considered a dear friend. Robin Combe spent many hours with my father and was a lively and eccentric presence throughout my childhood. It was Robin who came in the early hours of the morning when we got the call from the hospital on 15th January 1986 to say my father had lost his life to cancer, after a mercifully short illness. It was Robin who came to our wedding on a small island in the middle of the Thames and - with the honesty that befits his character - expressed his doubts about me having been taken me out of the local school aged thirteen at my desire to be home educated, whilst at the same time reassuring my new husband and inlaws that - despite his reservations about my dubious educational career - "she hasn't turned out too badly."

It is Robin who welcomes my family regularly with our caravan so I can reconnect with my roots in Blakeney and North Norfolk. It is Robin who invites us all in for 'bath night' when we've been camping for a few days and are (in his words) "getting a bit whiffy".

And it is Robin who has always encouraged us in our boating life choice, and has persistently told me I should write up our life on board. I can't help feeling that he is standing in the footsteps of my father in so doing. The only comment I remember my father making regarding my career choices - I was only twelve when he died - was him saying 'you might be a writer one day'. (He was a great writer himself, having been in the advertising world prior to becoming a watercolour painter.)

For the last ten years I have been writing play scripts for our youth theatre company, 'Fusion'. To misquote my younger self; 'I'm used to this'. But thanks to Robin and his constant prompting, and the never-ending influence of my father in all aspects of my life, I am about to embark on a more 'slip-sliding in the Blakeney mud / I'm not used to this' sort of challenge.

My family and I have lived on our sailing barge Golden Mean on the Thames for six years and then on the Norfolk Broads for twelve years. Our lifestyle is generally viewed as out of the ordinary. Although we are used to it, there is something about living aboard that never becomes ordinary, even for us. Since 2003, our 50 foot sailing barge has played a central part in our lives and our life decisions. She is our home, our office, our schoolroom, our church, our place of safety. She is the birthplace of our second child, she is the vehicle and accommodation of our holidays, our days out with friends, our hospitality, a piece in the community jigsaw of where we live.

It is my hope to reflect honestly and openly the stories of our lives on board in a way that gives an insight into some of our life choices, why we've chosen the paths we have and why we keep going that way. It is my hope that these insights might inspire others to dare to do things differently. To leave the safety of the harbour for the literal and metaphorical freedom and challenge of the open seas.

Chapter 1: In the beginning

"Samaritans, can I help you?"

Nothing.

Again, more softly, more encouraging;

"Hello, Samaritans, can I help you?"

Nothing.

{Pause}   "I'm glad you rang. Is there something worrying you that you wanted to talk about....?"

Nothing.

Then a small voice;

"I don't really know where to ... I don't know if I can .... oh, I can't do this - ". {Phone clicks off}

Before I've got a chance to record the scant vital statistics of that call, the phone rings again. I try to muster my most compassionate tone, hoping to draw her out more this time.

"Samaritans, can I help you?"

A male voice this time, with a deep Glaswegian accent; "Shall I tell you what I'd like to do to - "

I have a rough idea where this might be going, but I'm obliged to continue for now, so I interrupt slightly:-

"This the Samaritans..." (there's an infinitesimal chance he dialed the wrong number unknowingly), "...can I help you, is there something you want to talk about?"

{An unpleasant chuckle}

It's 3am on Saturday morning. My co-volunteer's phone rings and I can hear that his caller sounds like my previous one ringing back again. It is a lottery as to who picks up any call – it might not even be the same branch. One of the deliberate technical choices of the charity, in order to discourage attachments to individual volunteers. I try and focus on my call in an objective way:

Caller: "Are you still there sweetheart?"

Oh dear. Sometimes silence is best policy. He isn't put off by the silence. He sounds like he's had a bevvy or two, and says:

"Are you on your own, shall I – "

I interrupt. It's worth a try.

"I'd rather talk about your emotions, what prompted you to call The Samaritans this morning ... "

I can tell by his breathing his prevalent emotion is now anger. But there are certain topics that are off limits, even to a non-judgmental befriending service like the Samaritans and I've got enough experience to make a few assumptions.

"Oh, XXXX you!" he shouts, and hangs up.

I'm not doing very well. We're supposed to ask every single caller if they are suicidal, ideally fairly early in the conversation. I've failed – for different reasons - to draw these two callers out. Thomas, my co-volunteer on this night shift, is doing better. I can hear that he's 'popped the question' and from the one side of the conversation, it sounds like the answer was in the affirmative and he's 'steering into the pain', as we are taught to do. I leave the phone room to make us both a cup of tea. I tried to do this a couple of hours ago but the phone kept ringing. Which is why I'm here; to talk to those in desperate distress, often with nobody else to turn to, and try and offer a non-advisory befriending ear.

Thomas always jokes that on night shifts, the more tired I became, the more manic my behaviour. In between calls I'd be doing the filing, cleaning or washing up. There are two types of Samaritan volunteers on a night shift. The one who catnap between calls, and the one who stay manically awake at any cost. I'm in the latter category. I'm not one of those people who is blessed with the ability to convince the early morning caller that they haven't just woken me up. Frankly, I sound (and feel) groggy for at least an hour (and a cup of coffee or two) after waking. Always have.

The dreaded night shift occurs once in every eight weeks of more civilized daytime shifts. In truth the nights are more rewarding, especially the first half from 11pm – 2am, which are usually busy and full of 'serious' callers. So on these shifts I prefer to stay fully awake - which means lots of coffee and pottering about the office in between calls. Thomas, on the other hand, is happy to doze whenever there is a quiet period and is able to answer within three rings sounding composed and not in the least bit groggy. (I was once looking after someone's dog and brought it with me on a night shift - and I was terribly worried the caller would be able to hear its snores!)

Mercifully our Glaswegian friend hasn't called back, he's probably onto another branch now. You can't blame him, it's free to call and you're guaranteed a friendly sympathetic voice, that is quite likely to be female. Technically, we're not supposed to hang up. But there are ways of 'discouraging' someone who is basically abusing the service and also blocking genuinely distressed callers from getting through, as indeed there are techniques to draw them out. That's what the training is for.

It's really excellent and sometimes I think it should be a compulsory life skill.

I finish the tea and grab a plate full of bourbons and place some in front of Thomas who by now is deeply ensconced in a heavy conversation. I place his non telephone hand on the mug handle and indicate the biscuits. He gives me the thumbs up. He's now got the challenge of trying to eat a bourbon silently.

In early 2002, when Thomas and I were doing our nightshift, the Putney branch of The Samaritans occupied a tatty first floor of 106 Felsham Road. I have the fondest memories of my six years volunteering and helping with training and administration. Friendships with other volunteers that lasted a lifetime, not least members of my own training group from May 1997, which was a microcosmic representation of the eclectic mix of volunteers that the charity attracts. There was me, aged 26 and in between jobs, a Catholic priest, a 30 something juggling a career in HR with two young children, a salesman, an actor, a software executive, an editor - and those were just some I got to know well. It was a splendid example of people from all walks of life coming together for a common purpose. Aside from our weekly telephone and (more occasional) face to face shifts, our 'Class of '97' met monthly in the Kings Head on the river for socials and some of us did long distance fundraising walks and went to national conferences together. We even spent one weekend redecorating the call rooms. Volunteers are a real mixed bunch of genuinely good eggs. Although I would never have dreamed it would become a reality, I might reasonably have hoped to meet a kind, generous and caring chap through my years volunteering. When responding to the question of how we met, I like to add that it wasn't on opposite ends of the phone. Thomas likes to throw in that I was his trainer. Anyway, it was an auspicious start.

The decision to volunteer came soon after returning from a turbulent three month backpacking stint with a friend in Australia. I was still adjusting to life after travel, unenthusiastically looking for secretarial work and sofa surfing in the living room at my previous house share, as we had given away our rooms to a bunch of lively South Africans prior to globetrotting. It was an unsettled time in search of meaning and purpose.

For a month or two I had returned to the job I loved in a quirky Nursery School in Wandsworth, but that was short lived as the building had been sold to a housing developer and soon culminated in an emotional relocation for pupils, teachers and parents. This was followed by an unsuccessful stint at a more 'corporate' nursery in Twickenham, which in turn bounced me back into secretarial work, initially as a PA at a toy manufacturer in Clapham, and later as PA to the Manager of the Draughting Department at Earls Court Exhibition Centre. Although I could fill a chapter with stories of the more social interactions during my time there, the role just wasn't me. After reading the 'Which Career' guide in a bookshop during my lunchbreak on the Earls Court Road, I made the decision to apply to the Roehampton Institute to undertake a three year Primary Education degree. It was a career I had aspired to as a teenager, but studiously avoided due to the necessary business of attending University - an environment that seemed most unattractive when I was a home schooled teenager already settled in the adult world.

During my years in unfulfilling office work, Putney Samaritans successfully filled my need for altruistic purpose, personal challenge and friendship. Sadly, 106 Felsham Road was repossessed for renovation into smart apartments in the early 2000s. The branch moved further towards Putney High Street into a more modern unit. It never had quite the same attachment for me and combined with the move further out of town onto the boat in 2003, Thomas and I made the decision to pause volunteering for a time.

A few years later, after I had qualified as a teacher, I discovered that the old Earls Court Exhibition Centre had also been demolished. I'm sensing a pattern here. There is nothing like a building raised to the ground to make one feel nostalgic for the time spent there. Fond memories of playing badminton with the I.T. guys in empty exhibition halls and watching the set up for the Ideal Home and Boat Exhibitions, rehearsals for the Spice Girls Concert and the Royal Tournament, viewed for nothing during our 'smoke breaks' from the 'cheap seats' up on the fourth floor where I worked. Another era ended.

I first caught sight of Thomas when he came for an interview at the Putney branch. As well as volunteering, I was also involved in the administration side of the charity, and in that capacity had the advantage of having read his application (amongst others). Angela, who was the Director at the time, left the interview room, and I caught a glimpse of the back of Thomas disappearing down the stairs, flicking open his folded up white stick like a light sabre as he disappeared down the stairwell, wearing an enormous khaki army coat with a huge fluffy collar. It was an odd first impression looking back, but seems to have been memorable. Angela's comment 'that's a very level headed young man' confirmed he would be suitable for starting the training course the very next day. Interesting, as I would be on the training team.

The icebreaker to the training involved people saying their name and something trivial about themselves. In another context, "I'm Tandem-ing Thomas, and I'm looking for someone to go tandem-ing with," might have been an unsuccessful chat up line. But there was something courageous and attractive about this surprising one-liner delivered by a blind man to a room full of Samaritans and would-be Samaritans. From Thomas' weak vantage point, they were a room full of people of indeterminate age, gender, background, with varying degrees (or none) of suitability for tandem cycling - or indeed anything else Thomas might have needed help with for that matter. He kindly shared in the group round-up at the close of the day that he'd had 'some interest' in the tandem thing. He later admitted that I was in fact the only person who had expressed an interest in sharing his tandem during the tea break, whilst simultaneously plying him with ginger nuts - whereupon he told me that the tandem had paniers and could carry a tent - which I frankly thought a little forward, given we'd just met.

In my timely capacity as administrator/trainer I proceeded to type up the post-session handouts which conveniently had never been put into electronic format. A job that was frankly long overdue, and one that enabled Thomas to access the notes with his screen-reader. This naturally required a professional follow-up email after each of the six sessions with the electronic handouts, which included a little 'chat', which perhaps became a little less than professional as the weeks went by.

Halfway through Thomas's training course the fiancé of one of my close friends from teacher training was stabbed in a car jacking incident in Battersea and died in hospital a few days later. This was naturally a huge trauma to my friend and the ripple effect included her immediate family and friends, of which I was a part. We were a small group of mature students who had gravitated together on the course and spent time together socially too. It was a really sad and difficult time. I remember one of the other Samaritan trainers asking me if I 'should be here?' for the training session that evening, knowing what was going on in the background. I think I replied that it was helping me to keep my mind occupied. Nobody was about to send me home from a group of Samaritans.

It was the oddest of times to begin dating, but that's what transpired. I suppose it wasn't that odd given we were all in the business of active and empathetic listening - which was what I needed at that moment. It took another six months before we got on the tandem, but we did achieve the London to Brighton Cycle race - twice - and on the first occasion, we actually made it up Ditchling Beacon without getting off!

Although this chapter has barely mentioned Golden Mean, I found I could not embark on tales of our life on board without talking about Putney Samaritans and the influence it had in our lives. Thomas found himself there because a friend of the family, a Benedictine monk who had also been his headmaster, suggested that he would be good at it and he should apply. A few years earlier, I had been flipping through the Yellow Pages in search of inspiration - I know it sounds unlikely, but this was pre-internet- and had found the Samaritans advertisement and called to enquire about training. Somehow, in a seemingly random way, our planets aligned in January 2002, and I thank God for that and all that has followed.

Chapter 2: Bricks and mortar, or steel and water?

I developed a slightly less extreme way of getting to know Thomas, prior to jumping on a tandem to go camping; I made sure I was always on hand to offer him a lift home after training. I remember looking meaningfully in the eye of a lovely volunteer called Tony, who lived quite near Thomas in Wimbledon and had offered him a lift, assuring him that "no, it really wasn't too much out of my way". Tony got the message and backed off, with a knowing smile. At the time I was driving a Diesel Peugeot 106. Thomas, with a distinct preference for diesel engines over petrol, made a mental note in my favour. Driving capabilities was the next yardstick.

With the lack of privacy afforded by our respective shared houses, and to ensure my driving was up to scratch on motorways and not just in the city, Thomas and I began to head out of London most weekends to spend them at his childhood home in East Sussex. The first weekend was the most memorable. Thomas decided to throw a party. He assured me that his friend Freddie, who had recently completed his 'Man in the Kitchen' course, would handle the catering. Thomas's parents would be away visiting his younger brother who was taking a gap year in New Zealand, but we would have access to their freezers which were allegedly brimming with leftovers from his sister's recent 21st.

It was an interesting weekend. Arriving at his parents' home for the first time with them absent seemed a little odd, although Thomas didn't seem to think so. The guests were dominated by 'ghosts of girlfriends past' - plus Freddie, who I liked enormously, but who definitely had no inkling that he had been nominated head chef.

These days I enjoy catering for friends and family in our little galley. Twenty years ago I hadn't much experience of having 'my own kitchen', as I shared a house with five others in Balham. As for many other 20-somethings in London, it was a transient existence. It was pretty unusual to have the whole kitchen to oneself, on the rare occasion I was home for supper. My flatmates joked that they didn't see me from one week to the next. I think the longest period I spent at the house was when I had glandular fever and couldn't get out of bed for three weeks.

In order to squeeze in two extra bedrooms on the ground floor, the communal space was crammed into a tiny living room at the back, with a minute kitchen which I think may have been even smaller than our boat one. I was designated the top middle cupboard for my food stores and one shelf (can't remember which) in the fridge. The turning knob on the hot tap broken long ago and been replaced by an adjustable spanner, which to Thomas - coming from a family where things got fixed the minute they were broken - had become a permanent feature. My housemate once had a mouse leap out of the toaster when he put his slice in. With 24 hour food stores on the doorstep and me out at Samaritans or at work, catering wasn't really a thing. During my six years in the house, as flat mates came and went, I gradually pulled rank over which room I occupied and settled on the first floor in a huge front room which became more of a bedsit, and housed a large sofa as well as my bed, desk and electric piano. It was a fun house, but 'in need of modernisation' as the estate agents put it.

Back to Sussex. Had I known I was catering for a bunch of Thomas's slightly over-protective female friends, all eager to scrutinize me out for suitability, I would have been more at ease starting from scratch and creating something of my own that would have at least given me kudos in the cookery department. Thomas, keen on finishing up leftovers, had other ideas. His mother's garage freezer was full of burgers, sausages and frozen baps. To him it was just a question of feeding people. He's grown up in a family with a mother who is extremely hospitable who welcomes guests of all sorts – invited or otherwise – to her kitchen table. Jenny does it with style, makes it look easy, everyone is welcome: masquerading as an extrovert, even though she'd probably rather be having a long bath or a solitary walk.

I can't remember what oddities we served up that night with me at the helm, but my lasting impression is embarrassment at the assortment of leftover party food on offer and under scrutiny from the female guests. Thank God for Freddie's calming presence. He and

Thomas were at school together, Thomas would later become his best man and Freddie godfather to our son Digby.

Mercifully, on our next escape to the country, Jenny and Graham were back from their travels and on arriving, Jenny greeted me warmly - without obvious scrutiny - whilst up to her elbows in something or other in the kitchen. Thomas and I played a duet on the piano, and before I knew it I was taking part in the initiation rite of any new visitor who claims to read sheet music; stumbling my way through 'Easy come, easy go' and 'I cover the waterfront' from the Johnny Green songbook. For someone who doesn't play an instrument, Graham is a surprisingly big and knowledgeable fan of music - especially jazz. My brother in law Dominic, who can play the piano superbly without having done any grades and with only nine fingers, plays much better than me; with my Grade 8 and infuriating inability to play much at all without a piece of music in front of me. I think I made a good enough fist of the sight reading to satisfy my future father-in-law that another pianist was joining the family – if not an extrovert one.

Shortly after starting with the Samaritans, Thomas had also started a new job with London Underground, so with me half way through my teaching degree, we were both committed to London for the time being. Weekend escapes to Sussex became a regular feature of our new relationship. Thomas enjoyed the independence that public transport within London afforded him but I, having been in London some 15 years already, relished the chance to relive my countryside roots. It gave us both a break from respective flat mates, not to mention unlimited use of a large kitchen with taps that work properly. (Everything works properly at Finches, because Graham is nothing short of a genius when it comes to fixing things.)

Thomas spent many idyllic childhood summers messing about on and off boats on Eilean Shona, an island off the West Coast of Scotland where his Aunt and Uncle lived. With teenage siblings and slightly older cousins, a wide selection of floating craft and the tidal Loch Moidart on the doorstep, he well and truly caught the boat bug. The idea of living aboard came up in conversation more frequently, although if he meant us living on board together, I hadn't caught on. As an interesting way to pass the time one weekend, I agreed to go along with him to visit his friend on her narrow boat.

We embarked at Marylebone station and, with the navigation stresses that have become a feature of our lives, we somehow found our way fairly unharmoniously to a dingy canal surrounded by grey graffiti covered concrete. As I was sketchy about some of the facts whilst recalling this, I asked Thomas how he knew where to find his friend's boat. He tells me that he had been on a previous occasion, in order to help her move her boat through a tunnel to Little Venice, to empty her sewage tank. Presumably this was a planned event where his assistance was welcome, unlike the occasion that we visited together, uninvited. We finally found the boat, having stepped over rickety narrow walkways and Thomas insisting on using his white stick. Me thinking, and possibly articulating, how ridiculous was the notion that Thomas could possibly habit such an environment safely.

In retrospect, I have complete sympathy. The friend was trying to replace her cooker, or washing machine, or something domestic. Anyone that's been on a narrow boat knows that they are thus named for a reason. They are six feet ten inches wide and passing in the corridor is only possible if you are on intimate terms. Made of steel, their lack of width means that when you step on (or off) you are likely to wobble the boat to the degree of sea-sickness. I'm exaggerating of course, but the narrow width does make them less stable than something with a wider beam. She, surprised by our visit and clearly right in the middle of a fix, was neither able nor inclined to welcome us into her home. After a brief conversation we were on our way back across the maze of mismatching boardwalks back to Marylebone station. I can't remember the detail of the rest of that day, but it's likely I dragged Thomas into a coffee shop to recover.

Things went a bit quiet on the boat front after that, although the weekends in Sussex continued. I was approaching my finals and in a challenging school placement in Croydon. One Sussex escape weekend in the early Summer of 2003 proved to be a pivotal moment in our lives. My mother Partridge, who lived in Chelsea at the time, came down by train to join us in Sussex for Sunday lunch. She had bought a Sunday Times on the station and she settled on the sofa to read it after lunch. I suppose we must have mentioned something to do with boats prior to this, otherwise it was a complete coincidence that she read out an article in the Sunday Times Magazine about a couple who, in their retirement, had bought a narrow boat and now spent their time cruising the UK waterways. The title; the same as this chapter. It piqued our interest.

There was something else that had piqued my interest. The growing realization that our conversation had now developed from Thomas living on a boat to us living on a boat together. The article mentioned an annual boat show in Northampton and a rapid google search told us that by remarkable good fortune, the Crick Boat Show was coming up later that month. With the typically cavalier attitude of two un-marrieds, we jumped on the idea and made a plan to head to Northampton for the bank holiday weekend.

I have a particular knack for forgetting details that are not significant. The Crick boat show, although highly significant in the sequence of decision making leading up to moving aboard Golden Mean, does not feature highly in my memory. I remember stepping onto a narrow boat and feeling that this would be a very enclosed space for two people to live. I remember a burger van on a hot dusty field. The cataclysmic moment was discovering a type of boat called a wide beam barge - similar in style to a narrow boat but double the width. The brand new barge that we viewed at the show really blew my mind in terms of what a living space on a boat could be like. Erase your image of a damp, dark, cold and cramped space; this was light and bright with large windows all around a generous open plan living space with a fireplace and large L-shaped sofa. The two double bedrooms were spacious and comfortable and the boat didn't tip when you stepped on or off. This was something else. This was something we could really live on and make our home; together. I was excited. All sorts of possibilities were stirring in my mind.

As the Summer heated up I found myself in central London in a hotel having a ghastly interview for a teaching agency, near Trafalgar Square. After my interview, feeling hot, bothered and uncomfortable in a suit, I trailed the newsagents looking for a particular magazine that, based on its absence, was apparently not that popular. 'Waterways World', we were told, was the place to look for boats for sale. Eventually I sourced one and, meeting Thomas in the park during his lunchbreak, we sat on the grass and I began to scan the 'For Sale' section.

We had talked about it at length since the boat show and agreed that a modern wide beam barge would be lovely. We wanted to be able to take her out on trips and we judged that 60 feet would be the minimum length that would be big enough to live on but small enough to manoeuvre around the Thames. We had some savings - but we didn't want a massive debt and marine mortgages are difficult to get. So it was going to be something second hand and we would have to negotiate a good price. So, 60-70 foot in length, wide beam barge. Basically a floating caravan with an engine to go for gentle cruises at the weekends. Nothing complicated. Nothing seaworthy.

It must have been another shift of fate that led me to read the advertisement on the Virginia Currer Marine page out to Thomas, because as you can see it really wasn't what we were looking for. I contemplated not reading it out loud. But I did read it, sitting on the grass in St James's Park in the hot midday sun eating grapes. I still have the page:

"All steel 15.2m (50ft) x 4.1m (13.4ft) Gaff Rigged barge yacht, commissioned 1995. Designed by Alan Hill. 2 x Sabre 80hp diesels. 4kVA diesel generator. 4/6berths. 2 permanent double berth cabins with convertible double in saloon. BSC to 10/2003."

---

50 feet? Not big enough. A sailing barge? Too complicated - Thomas would want to sail the blessed thing. Price was too high and it didn't say where it was located. Too late now. We phoned the agent, spoke to John Currer whose first question as prospective liveaboard boat owners was 'Do you have a mooring?' Er; well no, actually we hadn't thought about that yet.

Cue another trip to north London, this time to Perivale to have a look at the Grand Union Canal which passes through. We had read that liveaboards could stay on free moorings on canals for two weeks at a time before having to move on. Perhaps we could be gyrovagues? The canal was dirty and teaming with mosquitos. We walked along a towpath but there was nothing to suggest this would be a suitable or even desirable place to live for two days, let alone two weeks. Never mind, we'll cross that bridge later.

Another weekend jaunt. We got on the train at Clapham Junction and headed for Staines. I introduced Thomas to Starbucks iced frappes and we wandered along the river. The Thames is very wide here and the houses between Staines and Chertsey locks are, on the most part, large and pricey with expansive gardens running down to the river. The towpath is excellent and we walked as far as Penton Hook Lock, keeping an eye out for - what, exactly? In our naive position I think we hoped to see a sailing barge along the towpath with a 'for sale' sign in the porthole. But nothing like that, so we wandered back to our respective flat shares.

Our next port of call was to arrange a viewing with the agent, who kindly agreed to pick us up from a nearby railway station and take us to the marina, which we discovered was a good couple of miles walk from the station back in the direction of Chertsey. Penton Hook Marina is a large floating boat park. They had a decent chandlery, run by Steve who also lived on a boat and had spent six months cruising through the French waterways. Behind the chandlery, an old fashioned yacht club which allegedly separated its male and female members into gender segregated circles at socials, which we never frequented, except for when we undertook our Day Skipper theoretical training some years later. Staff were friendly and there was a toilet block and a laundry. John Currer pressed us on where we might be keeping the boat and when we asked; 'Could we not continue to moor her here?' he seemed surprised, but this later proved to be the solution and we wondered why he hadn't suggested it.

John led us down a long pontoon to what's known as the hammerhead; the T shaped pontoon across the end. It was a hot July day, the evocative smell of hot water and hot boats still drifts back to me sometimes on hot summers days on our pontoon in Norfolk. This was our first sighting of Golden Mean, then an eight year old gaff rigged sailing barge. Her substantial mast, made of Canadian Douglas Fir, was currently lying almost horizontal along on the deck, resting in a specially purposed bracket just above the railings on the stern. With her black hull and striking red stripe, she outshone all the other boats in the marina. I tried to explain the visuals to Thomas, which is always difficult when you're looking at something complicated and bespoke. What could I liken her to? There is no comparison. He has to grab at each strand of detail as it emerges, feel his way round, 'seeing with his hands' as he puts it. He has to find out for himself, slowly, over time, by feel and experience and with some help from the limited powers of description from friends and family.

Designed by professional Alan Hill for sailing enthusiast Steve Kenworthy, and built in Steve's Lancashire barn over five years, Golden Mean is the epitome of handcrafted uniqueness. A far cry from the off the peg straightforward wide beam barge that we had decided would suit us, this boat has an enormous amount of Douglas Fir Tree on her deck, lashings of stainless halyards, stays, pulleys, winches, tackle and coils and coils of rope that all have a special meaning and purpose when she comes to life as a sailing vessel. She has an enormous stainless steel wheel in the cockpit, as well as an optional wooden tiller if you want to do it the traditional way. Her tan mainsail covers 1150 square feet. There are three sails; the mainsail - enormous and flanked at the top by the gaff, a smaller wooden boom that pulls the sail up at a sharp angle to reach higher than the mast itself, which is a topped with a red flag. The smaller tan sail, the stay sail, goes in front of the main sail. Finally, there is a white sail which attaches to the end of the bowsprit which can be extended out from the front of Golden Mean some 10 feet or so, this is the furling headsail. All very complicated. Thomas is not the sort of person to live on a sailing barge and never sail her. He's sailed at University and he'll want to get those sails up. And at 50 feet she is surely too small to live on?

On that first viewing, the cockpit was entirely open to the elements, with a self draining floor for when the waves roll over. Just before our first child was born, we encased the cockpit in canvas and essentially created another room; used for dining, schoolwork, lego, keeping dry during voyages and storing of logs in the Winter. To enter the cabin of the boat, you climbed down a set of stairs akin to a ladder, where the main cabin is about a metre lower than the cockpit. The ladder style steps have been replaced in the last few years by our brilliant carpenter friend Peter, with a more gently sloping set of steps to accommodate Thomas's first guide dog Magic in his latter years when arthritis had set in. People used to ask how Magic coped with the steep ladder staircase. For most of his life, he simply missed it out completely and jumped up, or down.

Downstairs we discovered an open plan kitchen/living area. To the right, the navigation cupboard and fold down chart table are now used as a desk space, with electric piano and a laptop. Dining can be seated at a table, when it happens and usually with guests, in the now enclosed cockpit and mostly in the Summer months - although we did host Christmas there for ten round the table, pre-children. Downstairs, the galley to the left houses a full sized gas cooker/hob, work surface flanked with terracota tiles, stainless steel sink and a small microwave. At the time, the fridge/freezer was located under the work surface through a hatch. We later replaced this with a conventional fridge in another cubby hole and put a washing machine under the counter. The saloon has two very comfortable reclining leather armchairs and a sofa bed. There is a woodburning stove and loads of storage built into the walls. The teak and oak woodwork, and there is lots of it, is beautifully crafted. Seven portholes run down each side of the hull and they decrease in size gradually from the back to the front. There are also seven opening roof hatches, which shed plenty of light into the cabins.

Down the corridor on the right we find a tiled wet room - later replaced by less leaky fibreglass. This contains a pumping sea toilet, shower and basin. There are two double cabins, one with a sink on the port side and another in the bow. Bunks are later built into both of these by the ever-practical father in law, so that we can rearrange our growing family as appropriate.

We will return a couple more times before we begin to negotiate the price, with more useful engineering know-how in the form of Thomas's father and Uncle Stuart, who eschew the engine room with pleasure and all the practical what-nots that don't actually interest me right now, because I'm not thinking about sailing or even driving the boat. This is somewhere that we could actually live. In the end we only ever viewed the one boat. However more sensible and practical a floating caravan might have been, the decision was, from the first moment we stepped aboard, unequivocally Golden Mean.

On 5th August 2003, two months after viewing the advertisement in St James's Park, we completed the last of several trips back and forth from Staines to Balham with my little Peugeot stuffed full of my bits and bobs. I can't remember loading up Thomas's room in Wimbledon, I expect he just had a rucksack. Desperate to start our onboard adventure, we were determined to fit every last bit of my collectables in that last trip, which included my full size electric piano. This meant that poor Thomas spent the last journey crouched on the floor in the passenger foot-well, so intent we were on this being the very last trip. The boat's Eberspacher diesel boiler had packed up (not for the last time) but it didn't seem to matter because it was so hot that cold showers were quite acceptable for the two weeks it took to get it fixed. It was like an exotic camping holiday. I wish I could remember what we had for our first meal on board our first home.

Our immediate boating neighbours, another liveaboard couple on a very smart replica Dutch barge called 'De Vrowe Panacea', had been observing our comings and goings, and were soon to become good friends and allies in the boating adventure. Mike would sit alongside me as I took Golden Mean out for the first time, beginning with the hardest part; maneuvering around the crowded marina basin. There was a small lake nearby which we dubbed 'the playpool' and was the perfect place to practise without fear of collision. When we'd found our sea legs we'd explore further, turning left through Penton Hook lock and heading upstream towards Windsor and Cookham - where we got married in 2005, with Golden Mean moored on an island for our reception party. Or turn right to Chertsey lock and downstream to Shepperton and towards tidal Thames at Teddington. We wouldn't get that far until we were ready to leave London for our big voyage north in 2009.

Before too long, we'd be curious enough to raise the mast for the first time and learn about the sailing rig. Thomas's colleagues came down for an evening out and, outside The Swan in Staines, watched by some stunned summer evening revelers, we winched Andy, Thomas's then boss who was a keen sailor, to the top of the mast in a bosun's chair to adjust some pulley that had ended up in the wrong place. On another occasion I winched Thomas up the mast to fiddle with something or other, narrowly avoiding killing him when I mistakenly unwound the rope completely from the winch in order to lower him down, which meant I was then holding his full weight as I struggled to get the rope back on the winch. Luckily there was a second 'safety' line attached. Some Canadian geese passed by underneath him.

Returning from the hour's commute to central London, we'd often head straight to the 'playpool' to mess about in the dinghy. We'd take Golden Mean down the river for weekends, nearby to the Laleham Reach, just for a change of scene and to enjoy the towpath walking, or further afield through locks to Chertsey, Shepperton, Runnymede, Windsor and Cookham. Mostly joined by friends and family, some who stayed overnight as pre-children we had a spare bedroom and a sofa bed at our disposal. There is undoubtedly something of the holiday feel about living aboard, even when you've done it for years.

I spent six years living with, or perhaps more accurately, 'alongside' others in an often-changing dynamic of personalities in the terraced house at Balham. It wouldn't be fair to say that some of those housemates didn't become good friends, although I haven't kept in touch with any of them very well. I pretty much lived in my room and we were often ships passing in the night. When you live on board an actual ship (technically Golden Mean is a ship) there is no avoiding getting to know those you live with intimately. Even on a big boat, it's an undeniably smaller space than the average family home. But more on that later.

Suffice to say, that there are pros and cons of the liveaboard life, high moments and low ones. Being moored securely to a floating pontoon in a sheltered marina is relaxing; but when out on the tidal river and things go wrong, it can become very tense. You have to enjoy both; a good metaphor for a healthy marriage perhaps. We've been on board nearly eighteen years which means this is the longest time I've lived anywhere - having left home at seventeen. That doesn't mean we aren't still finding new things out about each other, why we choose the life we do - and about our vessel. Thomas sometimes says there is a difference between why we chose to live on a boat, and why we choose to stay on it. I hope to expand on that in subsequent chapters.

Chapter 3: Tales of the Thames

My father in law of a matter of hours calls "Bye Robin, bye bye!", one of the phrases now immortalised in a folder on my hard drive entitled 'Wedding clips'. My godfather Robin and his wife Kim are on board 'The Maite', a chunky red and white day boat, who has 'seen a lot of action', and now putt-putts her way along the Cliveden Reach in the setting sun. The Maite, hired from a chap the other side of the lock with the strict instruction: 'maximum capacity of 8 persons', is currently overflowing with twelve or more wedding guests and captained by my new brother-in-law William. She splutters her way doggedly back and forth from the small National Trust island where Golden Mean is moored downstream to Islet Road; where most of the guests left their cars earlier this afternoon.

After a small and personal wedding service in Holy Trinity Church, Cookham, many of the guests had jumped into The Maite, who waited patiently, festooned with ribbon and balloons, on the pontoon we had borrowed from a kind resident. Nearly eight year old Isobel; my only bridesmaid and former pupil, sat on the bow between Thomas and I. A few guests chose to walk along the towpath in the shade of the woods that had become so familiar to us during our many weekends and holidays on 'our island' over the past two years. The walkers still needed to be ferried across the channel of water - marked on the ordinance survey as 'Slow Grove' - to the island, either in The Maite or in our dinghy with its electric outboard. In order to fulfil the obligations stipulated by the Church of England for getting married at a church which is not your local one, we had to be 'resident' in the parish for at least six weeks. This is one of those occasions, like flooding, when we're glad we live on a boat. We did indeed reside on Slow Grove for six weeks; in the early Summer prior to our wedding in July, commuting daily from Maidenhead to our respective jobs in central London. Our marriage certificate holds a unique address; Golden Mean, Slow Grove, Cookham.

Jerome K. Jerome, in 'Three Men in a Boat' (1889), describes the Cliveden Reach as "…unbroken loveliness this is, perhaps, the sweetest stretch of all the river…" The Cliveden Reach was the inspiration for Kenneth Grahame's classic 'Wind in the Willows'. One of the larger islands was used by the Dutch Barge Association as the venue for their annual gathering - which we gatecrashed once, by dinghy. We met some delightful people, including a couple called Jenny and Alan to whom we gave a lift back to the mainland after the party. They had just had a new barge commissioned and, presumably planning on cruising the French Waterways, they proudly told us they were going to name her after themselves 'Jen-et-Al', which has made us chuckle on many occasion since.

Many boat owners we have met who have travelled that way have noted this short stretch between Boulter's Lock at Maidenhead and Cookham Lock as something a bit special. Heading upstream through the lock and leaving the suburbs of Maidenhead behind, you enter a watery paradise; a wonderland of woods, wildlife and islands. It was October half term when we first made it as far as Cliveden, with my future mother-in-law Jenny on board. As we came out of the lock I remember being struck by the magnificent Autumnal colours, the trees up the steep cliff on the Cliveden side reflected in glassy water. To the West, splendid views across open arable land and the towpath which takes you to the pretty village of Cookham, of Stanley Spencer fame. On the Easterly boundary densely wooded cliffs lead up to the grand Grade 1 listed country home Cliveden House, notorious as the setting for the 'Profumo affair' in the 1960s. Cliveden House is now an expensive hotel, and the grounds and woodland leading down to the river are managed by the National Trust and are beautiful and completely accessible - especially by boat. From the island you could swim it - or it's a tiny hop in the dinghy if you want to stay dry. It is also possible to moor on the Cliveden side at the bottom of the woods and a steep winding path will take you up to the house. On one of our frequent visits to the Cliveden Reach we thought it would be nice to take my friend Natasha, who was visiting for the day, to tea at Cliveden. I called ahead to check opening hours, only to be told that I would need to book for tea - two weeks in advance! Undaunted, we walked through the woods to the estate and visited the perfectly decent National Trust cafe in the grounds, where we had a somewhat more relaxed tea, not having to worry about whether or not the milk goes in first.

On our first landing on the island we were visited (by boat of course) by a National Trust ranger who had come to collect the overnight mooring fee of £6. On further enquiry, it became clear that we may purchase a season ticket for a modest £30 which would cover us for a whole year. The slightly bemused ranger agreed that, yes, if we so wished, we could stay as long as we wanted for that price. Knowing that we would be frequenting this little gem of a place at every possible opportunity, we hurriedly paid the £30 and thanked God for such a blessing.

One of the things that distinguishes hire boaters from boat owners, is that hire boaters tend not to stay very long in one place, preferring to cover as much of the waterways as possible in their allotted holiday time. I suppose the ranger had never encountered someone who considered the island an ideal spot to stay for a week - or several. The only practical hurdle to staying longer would be that we would run out of fresh water at some point, the nearest watering point being back through the lock. This we overcame by negotiating with Michael, of the aforementioned Islet Road, who generously invited us to moor at the bottom of his garden and use his hose to fill our tanks. I don't think he realised that we had six large tanks on board, as the filling took some considerable time. "How many tanks?" We duly recompensed him with wine.

On the three days following our small wedding, we invited other friends to join us on the island for continued celebrations. It was neither practical nor desirable to have everyone at the same time – and it made for a very intimate wedding. We were blessed with four days of glorious weather – which was fortunate as we didn't really have a wet weather plan and the island wasn't big enough for a marquee – just a small gazebo to serve Sangria from. So on 17, 18 and 19th July 2005, an assortment of friends and family arrived and squashed into The Maite with their picnics to celebrate with us. Our wedding list was bespoke – practical items we needed for the boat, such as camping chairs and a boathook. Whoever purchased the boathook – it's still in service. One such item was gifted by a very old friend, Tilly, in the form of a large parasol. In those days Golden Mean's cockpit was still open to the elements, but we erected Tilly's parasol at a jaunty angle which provided some shade over the cockpit. Thomas's mother had sewn some 'Just Married' banners which were hanging on both sides of the boom; Golden Mean fully rigged for the occasion. The banners encouraged many a toot from passing boaters. Our marina neighbours Mike and Lindsay moored alongside us on De Vrowe Panacea on our wedding day, heading off the next day. Guests came and went, we jumped off the boat, swam around and picnicked on the island and drank sangria on the deck. The sun beamed down. My friend Fr Vivian Boland, a Catholic Priest I had met on Samaritan training, travelled with us to the island, concelebrated with the local vicar at the service and blessed the boat with Lourdes holy water. When we somewhat reluctantly left the island a couple of weeks later to explore further upstream, with our 'Just Married' banner still up, a young family bought us icecreams in Cookham lock.

Whilst the Cliveden Reach was seven locks from home, and required us to invest more than a weekend to enjoy her many delights, Windsor - only four locks upstream - was an easier weekend trip. We would turn left out of our marina, past the weir and into Penton Hook lock. Provided you didn't arrive at lunchtime, there would be a friendly lock keeper on hand to handle the gates. All that remained for us to do then would be to throw a rope around a bollard on the shore, at bow and stern, and gradually let out rope, or take it in, depending on whether travelling downstream or up. Were you to naively make the rope fast to the bollard and go below deck to make a cup of tea, you'd risk your boat getting stuck midair as the water level drops away from the bollard. The lock keepers have seen it all. The scariest lock I have encountered was on the Canal Du Midi in southern France, on our busman's holiday with our respective families when Digby was nine months old. When the sluice gates underwater in the lock door were opened, such a volume of water rushed in, it was like being in a rapid.

Unlike English locks, you were expected to keep your engine on – and I can see why.

Travelling upstream from Penton Hook, you pass the lesser known back gardens of Staines (prettier than the front) and past the Swan pub. We once made the short trip to The Swan at night on my birthday in late November, having picked up our crazy Zimbabwean friend and his aged mother from his house on the riverfront at Laleham. We were waiting on anchor outside his house for longer than we anticipated whilst he took a leisurely bath. Prior to the cockpit being covered, I was layered up for driving with said friend and a brother in law on the bow keeping look out for obstacles in the river, notably buoys that are anchored to warn of shallow beaches along the river - but not lit. A lock is mighty deep and dark at night, and you have to operate the gates yourself. There was ice on the deck before we left the marina. Another brother in law and Thomas's sisters were also on board; inside the cabin with the woodburner going. We spent the night moored at the Swan, where we had drinks prior to a birthday meal in the excellent curry house behind the pub. We had a sprinkling of snow the next day for the return trip.

The next lock after Penton Hook is Bell Weir at Runnymede where the large taciturn lock keeper once persuaded my naive younger self not to bother tying up, as we were the only boat in the lock. It transpired that his motive was so that I was on the right side to pass him something from the other side, to save him the walk around the lock, meanwhile we incurred minor damage as we drifted into the lock wall. If you are going to collide with anything, especially something immovable, you'd better do it slowly. Something that the hire boaters would do well to remember. We were once hit on our mooring in Norfolk by a hire boat, which collided with our large anchors. Instead of stopping, they revved up, and promptly ripped a hole down the side of their hire boat.

Thomas's sister Tessa bought a house in Egham not long after we moved onto the boat and it was really fun having her nearby in those early days. We once picked up all the guests from a house party she was having, from the bank at Runneymede (of Magna Carta fame) and travelled back through Bell Weir lock - whereupon the same tricky lock keeper asked me if I had a commercial licence, there were so many people on board! I muttered something about the limit not including 'crew' and we passed through. At the next lock we kept most of the guests below deck.

After Runneymede comes Old Windsor Lock and then the village of Datchet where we once had a very stressful time trying to moor stern on. At the exact same spot a musician friend of ours proposed to his musician fiancé. So we remember the spot - but not fondly as they do. After Datchet comes Eton, where we visited one of specialist tailor shops to commission Thomas a silk waistcoat with embroidered anchors for our wedding, which he still wears to the occasional party. As we waited in the shop, families came in to order entire collections of very specific school attire, right down to dressing gowns, in preparation for their son's first term at Eton. The fourth lock is Romney which brings us into the centre of Windsor, and the usual mooring is on the recreation ground on the way out of town, from which you can walk into the historic centre with its' royal presence, tourist shops and proper Cornish pastie kiosk.

Often, very close to the 'official' mooring place, there is another landing spot that looks just perfect - perhaps a little further on under some trees with a stretch of secluded bank you can encamp to, or on the other side of the river from the madding crowd and likely with no mooring fee to be paid. But beware of these temptations as they can be a booby trap. On one such occasion, we moored on the opposite side of the river from the recreation ground at Windsor.

It looks attractive. There is a lovely open field where the dog can stretch his legs. There are already other (admittedly smaller) boats moored there but they'll probably move off at tea time and we'll have it all to ourselves. So we move in, find some handy trees to tie on to and put the kettle on. A few hours goes past and it's now too late to find another mooring even if we want to. And then, because we're on inside of the bend, where the depth is more shallow, and with boating traffic coming and going and causing a wash, we find ourselves firmly aground!

At least it's not Wells or Blakeney where you could have to wait weeks for a higher tide to lift you off. Also, this is the Thames and there are plenty of tourist boaters making stupid mistakes all the time, so you're not so conspicuous. Except of course that we are not on a hire boat, we are on Golden Mean which is entirely different looking from every other boat on the river. I'm a female driver, which throws them for a start. Our vessel looks serious, seaworthy and a bit large for the river upstream. People tend to assume that you know what you're doing. Many a time I've been frustrated in locks needing help with the ropes, shouting lefts and rights to Thomas - who thankfully has a pretty good aim. A liveaboard who wrote of his trip through France in a narrow boat named these silent, vacant onlookers 'gongoozlers' and we've used the term ever since. It's so apt. They sit and they stare, they might even take a video. They eat ice cream. They say nothing. They never offer to help, especially when you're in difficulties.

If you go aground on a tidal river, such as the Norfolk Broads where we now live, you have two options at this point. One; stick it out until the next high tide and hope that you don't either rip the trees out of the bank, the cleats off the boat or tilt over so far that the furniture starts to move of its own accord. Two; attempt to release the ropes somehow and try and manipulate your boat into deeper water.

Option two works better with a light, fibreglass Broads cruiser, not a 30 ton steel barge.

Fortunately, although your pride is dinted, there are helpful souls around – as opposed to gongoozlers - who would jump at the chance to help you in your time of distress. With luck they'll do it humbly and not rub your nose in it. On this occasion in Windsor, it was a boat much bigger than us, 'The Queen of the Thames', who came to the rescue. She's a huge floating party boat that cruises the waterways late at night with youngsters dancing on the deck with music blaring. Actually quite annoying if you've gone for an early night, as it takes just long enough passing you to wake you up before it disappears round the next bend. Its' inhabitants during the day are more sedate, mostly octogenarians enjoying a gentle cruise, some classical music and a cream tea. Thomas had been in the shallows in his wetsuit for some time trying to 'rock and roll' Golden Mean off the bank, to no avail. (He reminded me of that, I had forgotten the detail, again). Time to hail the Queen of the Thames who gallantly towed us free. We'd learned our lesson. Or had we?

In the spirit of honesty promised in the prologue, I have to tell you that we went aground again a few years later on the tidal River Yare near Bramerton. We were on our first voyage to Norwich, having arrived in Norfolk earlier that year, and were planning on picking up my mother from Norwich Yacht Station, just opposite the railway. As well as our two very young children, we had my mother-in-law and her friend (a sailor) on board.

On the outward voyage with bridges to navigate our mast was still horizontal and we were under engine power. We found another of those 'pretty and secluded' moorings, just off the beaten track and very close to the 'official' mooring, with two large trees to tie on to. In our defense, we were aware of the potential tide issue and we diligently observed the rise and fall of the tide during the day: up and down it went and all seemed well. But in the middle of the night my mother-in-law came and woke me up and said that we were 'at a bit of a tilt'. I was sleeping across the width of the boat with my head towards the starboard side, and as I struggled to wake up I realised with mild panic, that yes, I was actually on quite a steep slope with my head pointing downhill! We looked at the ropes with torches, which were by now extremely tight on the trees, and there was nothing we could do other than wait for the tide to float us off again in a few hours. Luckily, no damage done. It was on the return journey that we put up all three sails at Herringfleet and sailed from Somerleyton back to the marina.

We learned a lot about how to handle Golden Mean on the Thames, as we spent a lot of time out on the river; sometimes just the two of us but often with friends who were only too willing to accompany us on exploratory missions. One such weekend we were joined by Freddie and his now wife Fiona and Freddie's colleague, Robert. We had a pair of walkie-talkies at the time, and no dependent minors, and it was a very jovial trip. Mooring up is very simple if you stick to one rule. Always moor into the flow of the river. Even if it's a tidal river and it feels like 'slack water', it's probably moving in one direction or another, enough to make a difference. As we were still novices we had yet to fully digest this rule.

Golden Mean is a twin engine boat, meaning that with practice she is more maneuverable than a single engine craft. However, some other large boats have a little subtle onboard assistance to make mooring up look effortless – and not require as much skill. A bit like the caravans that come with a remote control so you can slot into your space without knowing how to back a trailer, some boats have these extra features in the form of bow and stern thrusters. At the push of a button you can nudge the bow, or stern (or both) of your boat sideways. Without blowing my own trumpet, handling Golden Mean is a skill that I've developed over the eighteen years we've been on board and if I can say so myself, I've earned some respect.

The way that Thomas and I learned is best to moor (or unmoor) Golden Mean, which works well if it's just the two of us, is by using what's known as a bow spring. Firstly I bring in the bow right to the shore, slowly at a gentle angle to the shore. (I can't actually see the shore as it gets close as the bow is quite high up, but I guess how close we are and give Thomas a '3,2,1' – which he would say is more of a '3, 2, ... pause ...... and then a sudden ONE!). Thomas has a feel for the shore with his feet from his position sitting on the edge of the boat near the front where she starts to curve in to the sharp bow. He hops off with the bowline once we are close enough for him to drop onto the shore. This is quite an unnerving experience for me, or anyone else watching, as he effectively disappears from sight for a moment. I'm on engines - this might sound obvious but it has been suggested (by Robin, actually) that Thomas steers and I go on the bow and shout lefts and rights and handle the ropes. We've never actually tried this, as I'm the sort of person who can do things if I'm the one doing them but I find it much harder to articulate what I'm doing whilst I'm doing it. Anyway, our method has worked so far, without Thomas falling in or being squashed between the boat and the shore. If there happens to be a useful person on the shore who is able to take the rope from him without him having to get off, put it round the bollard and hand it back, that's fabulous, but you can't rely on useful people being in useful places at the right time; they're usually somewhere else.

Once the rope is secured around a bollard and Thomas has the tail end in his hand he can control the tension. In other words, the bollard takes the strain, not Thomas. Similar to using a winch. It's essential that he keeps the tension on the tail end. This can be done from the shore, or, if I can give him an accurate 'left' or 'right', he can throw the rope over a bollard and control the tension from the boat without having to get off. This is how we handled locks together on the Thames.

I can now use the engines to drive the stern in, which is effective even when windy and when trying to get into a tighter space. I drive Golden Mean forward slowly and steer away from the shore, and as the tension is taken on the front rope, this has the magical effect of bringing the stern in. As the stern nearly reaches the shore, I put the controls in neutral and, whilst momentum continues to bring the stern into the shore, I attempt to throw the stern rope over the bollard. This is where our method can fall down, as if I miss, then the inclination is for the stern to spring away from the shore whilst the bow is held in tight. My rope throwing isn't brilliant. Luckily these days I have an able seaman in the form of my daughter Celeste, who can handle the controls whilst I throw, or vice versa. I'm hopeful that Digby and Celeste will take over more boat handling in their teenage years, although they are both already competent enough to handle the controls for a time.

I suppose the slick way of mooring up, which would work fine for a smaller lighter boat that you don't mind bumping, is to slew alongside the shore, drop off a person at the bow and another at the stern and they can usually hold the boat against the shore. With our heavier boat, that is also our home, it's much more controlled if we use the bow spring method.

Back to Windsor. It's not tidal upstream of Teddington ('Tide-end-town') but there is a noticeable flow heading downstream, particularly in narrow places or when there has been lots of rain. There probably didn't appear to be much visible flow that day. We were heading downstream with the flow, however negligible, pushing us along. We tried the slick method. With the flow pushing us from behind, Freddie who had hopped onto the shore simply couldn't hold on to the rope. There aren't any brakes on a boat – so if the boat is held by only one rope from the bow the flow would push us sideways. So Freddie had to let go and was left on the shore.

There is always a danger now that the trailing rope gets left in the water and wrapped around the propeller. (This happened once at our current marina, due to my lousy throwing, and it took Thomas and a friend two weeks up to their armpits in cold water reaching through the weed hatches in the engine room trying to cut it free. I'm not elaborating on that story, as it's too embarrassing.)

I do an impressive turn in the river and go round for another go. This time it's Robert who jumps off, manfully tries to bring her in - fails and has to let go. So we try again for a third time, now throwing ropes to Freddie and Robert on the shore. I remember thinking I might end up being the only person left on board! I can't remember how we managed it in the end - but it was a lesson learned about always mooring into the flow, however puny it may seem.

Talking of flow, the Thames can have a surprising current, especially after lots of flooding. One of the most damaging incidents, not to Golden Mean but to our dinghy and our pride, happened very close to home at Laleham near Staines. We used to head out to the riverbank mooring at Laleham for a short cruise with friends or as a change of scene. We once had Christmas lunch moored there on the towpath, the year before Digby was born with ten family members on board. It was generally a short and easy trip to do with day visitors, not involving any locks. On this occasion we went down for a weekend on our own when Digby was about six months, consequently I think we were still a little sleep deprived. It was Winter and the river was running faster than usual. It was just the three of us on board. Digby wasn't much use as crew, strapped safely into his baby car seat in the cockpit, topped up with milk and hopefully calm and happy for the hour it would take to get home, into the marina and tie up. The dinghy with its electric outboard was being towed from the back of the boat, as it was in the days before we put davits on the stern to hang it.

There only being one of Thomas, we had two choices. Take the front rope off first - or the back one. We decided to take the front one off because we knew the front of the boat would come away from the shore quite quickly and we would then be able to untie the stern (which is lower in line with the shore so closer to the bollard) and head straight out of the mooring. On this occasion the bowline was tied onto the shore, so Thomas had to get off to untie it – which we now try to avoid. We vastly underestimated the power of the flow, because as soon as Thomas let the front rope go, the bow whipped away from the shore really fast and we ended up at almost 90 degrees to the shore. The dinghy disappeared between the boat and the shore and I was screaming at Thomas to 'Get on, get on!' which he fortunately managed to do. However, the flow was pushing the front out so hard that the back rope was extremely tight and there was no way he could untie it. We made a quick decision to cut it free with the sharpest tool to hand; our serrated bread knife – and simultaneously drive away hard with the engines before we were swept sideways downstream. The dinghy reappeared, broken (but fixable) but the outboard was lost. We went back by car to try and find it, but never did. Another lesson not to underestimate the power of the river.

I shall conclude what has turned into quite an adventurous chapter with one final lucky escape. We sometimes visited our Zimbabwean friend who lived just across the river from the Laleham mooring. One evening we joined him for a bbq in his garden which bordered the river. Digby was still being carted about in his bucket car seat and we prepared to leave in our dinghy to make the short row across the river back to Golden Mean. We were just about to push off from the bank when a speedboat came haring down the river, unlit, at top speed. Whatever stroke of fate delayed us from leaving only seconds earlier, I am grateful, as we may not have survived to tell the tale. It's very unlikely they would have seen us. Mark did catch up with the speedboaters though, and politely explained to them (using a certain direct African approach) that they would not be travelling at that speed and without lights again in the future.

Chapter 4: Space, the final frontier

We'd been living aboard for four years when we announced to our NCT group that we were expecting our second child. One of the other mums (assume Canadian accent for a moment) responded with honest incredulity: "Where're ya gonna put it!?" It's no wonder that she struggled to take our boat as a home seriously from her vantage point in a large modern new build; a temporary home which came hand in hand with her husband's globe-trotting career with a large American food manufacturer. Her spacious neutrally decorated house came with every modern convenience - but very little in the way of characterful personal effects; what we consider home comforts. When we had NCT meet-ups at her place we'd try especially hard not to grind mushed banana into the carpet or leave coffee stains on the cream furniture. Which wasn't all that relaxing with eight babies in tow.

On other occasions Thomas and I would be invited over to enjoy a 'Tassimo' coffee pod, she had a cupboard filled with confectionary; the perks of her husband's job. We joined in with her share of the swimming pool that came with the house once or twice - and roasted our babies in the jacuzzi. By society's standards, she had by the far the most luxurious home. But we know don't we, that however much advertising, media and peer pressure tell you otherwise, space, luxury goods and modern conveniences don't equate to happiness. The truth was she would often spend long lonely days on her own with the baby whilst her husband was away on business.

After nearly eighteen years on board, friends and family are getting more used to our liveaboard life choice, although when we meet new people they are full of questions. One of the most bizarre was someone asking how the guide dog went to the toilet on the boat? Since the perception of guide dogs is that they are super-canine and can pretty much master anything in life, we were tempted to say that he just uses the boat toilet and pulls the chain afterwards. I have genuinely been asked if I could cook on the boat, is it windy on the boat, and the all-time favourite; is it cold in the Winter? I patiently (sometimes not so patiently) explain that it is a small space which is well insulated and we have both a wood burner and central heating; it is in fact very easy not only to heat up the boat quickly when we've been out all day, but also to keep it warm.

Crazy assumptions aside, most people are genuinely curious about the way we live, in a home which is undeniably different from the norm. People find it difficult to picture the inside of the boat, and so are usually surprised when they do come on board as it is invariably not how they imagined. Some visitors take themselves on a tour of the boat straight away, which I find surprising as you would probably not think it socially acceptable to head upstairs to have a nose around the bedrooms when you go to someone's house for the first time.

Sometimes it's more subtle, asking our children to 'show us where you sleep' – which basically encompasses the rest of the boat. But that is the introvert in me talking, and I admit an intrinsic need for privacy from time to time.

We recently did quite a massive tidy up, including some outdoor jobs that needed doing, in readiness for a family coming on their first visit to Golden Mean, which involved lunch, a cruise and a swim in the river and supper. The dining table in the cockpit was emptied of a good deal of Lego construction and the van boot was used as a temporary shed. It was lovely to see Golden Mean de-cluttered, it reminded me of when we bought her. The children of the same family came back a few weeks later for a sleepover and, when I explained somewhat apologetically to the 9 year old boy that the boat was looking messier than last time he was here because [last time] we had tidied up a fair bit in preparation, he said;

'I always say to my Mum, I don't know why people do that; because then you don't get to see how they really live, do you?'

But children are so much less judgmental than adults, aren't they? And nine year old boys aren't remotely bothered if you've hoovered or not, and are much happier to see the cockpit table overflowing with Lego than empty. The four children left the two perfectly good bunks empty that night, in favour of camping on the floor of the living space, because it was more fun all being squashed in together.

The truth is that nobody really knows what living aboard is really like, because when visitors come then the boat can sometimes feel over crowded. When it's just the four of us on board it's easy to spread ourselves into our own private spaces if we feel like it. And I do think headphones are a brilliant invention. If I have the rare good fortune of a little time on board by myself - it may as well be a palace.

It is looking through the eyes of others that we understand that, while many things are essentially the same, there are elements of our lifestyle which are fundamentally different; and not all of them are obvious. In the beginning, we were an unmarried couple in our late twenties seeking a fun alternative to shared flats in London. Friends and family came bringing friends of friends and work colleagues, and visited for dinner, for day trips, weekend adventures, sleeping in the spare room, on the sofa bed and in the cockpit. My class of six and seven year olds found the idea that I lived on a boat intriguing; how indeed could I get to school? Thomas came to give a talk on blindness, letting them have a go with his white stick (pre guide dogs).

The boat environment suits Thomas. Maybe if I returned to those higgledy piggledy pontoons in Marylebone today, with hindsight, it wouldn't seem so ridiculous that Thomas could live there. The pontoons where we live are wide enough to safely navigate with a white stick or a guide dog. The interior of the boat is organised with life at sea in mind, which means that fixtures are usually fitted and everything has its' place. The crockery is held in place with pegs that keep plates from sliding out in a Force 8 and the glasses fit into secure holes within their recess. Things are designed to be kept ship shape and, if his family don't cause too much disarray, Thomas can find his way around the boat much more efficiently than in a large house; even the house where he grew up which he knows well. Thomas has inherited, or learned, his father's desire and talent for fixing things. What's more; he can do it blindfold. I never fail to be impressed when he swops our diesel boiler (the infamous 'Eberspacher') for another unit (which seems to happen a couple of times a year, at least) in the confines of the engine room. Although visiting boat buffs and mechanically minded male friends have used adjectives like 'spacious', 'clean' and 'big' to describe it, our engine room is somewhere I'd rather not be, other than for moral support in dire circumstances.

I finished my first year of teaching with an open invitation to my pupils to visit in the Summer holidays. Max came with his sketch book and went down to the engine room to draw the engines. Rebecca, whose home life was unsettled at the time, visited when we were moored near her home in Whitchurch. She drew all the porthole curtains and turned the boat into a cosy den. Isobel (who was also my bridesmaid) and her friend Katie came over for a weekend at Shepperton. Katie brought a jar of redcurrant jelly "in case we were having a Sunday roast". Again moored on an island, this time the larger Desborough Island, we sent them 'Golden Tickets' promising a nautical adventure. We played pirates, swam in the river and they made 'potions' on the deck with all the contents of my food cupboard. When their parents came to collect them after two glorious days on the river, we were all sad to say goodbye.

Digby Philip Harrison was born at St Peter's Hospital, Chertsey at 8.05am on 25th August 2006. We were well looked after by midwives who visited us on the boat during my pregnancy. We were aiming for a home birth and during that very hot August I spent some time in the paddling pool which we squeezed into the cockpit. Those drainage holes in the floor of the cockpit enabled us to tip the water out into the floor after I had finished wallowing and it would disappear down a pipe into the river. To cut a long birthing story short (Thomas delights in telling it but I do not) I was moved to the hospital by ambulance, after a long tiring labour at home, and Digby was born shortly after arriving. Suffice to say that getting off the boat in that condition was not easy! However, all was well and we were blessed with a big healthy baby boy. Digby and I spent one night in hospital and came home the following day. My mother stayed on board for a couple of weeks to help before returning to her home in South Africa. Now we are three living on board.

Although I stopped full time teaching at the end of that Summer Term, after my initial maternity leave I resumed teaching the Junior Choir for another year. Thomas dropped down to four days a week with London Underground so was able to help with Digby. Jenny would come for lunch on Wednesdays, and afterwards I would drive to Wandsworth for the hour's rehearsal, and back again. Sometimes Thomas and Digby would come with me and would chat to various colleagues in the staff room whilst I was teaching.

Our least efficient 'work commute' was when the first rehearsal of the term coincided with Golden Mean being moored as far as we would ever travel up The Thames, at Cliveden Hampden, not far south from Abingdon. We walked some way along the tow path to a tiny railway station and caught one of the infrequent trains into Paddington, then across London to Putney. The hour's rehearsal took up most of that day. In my full time teaching days I kept a bicycle near Putney station and cycled across to the school after the commute in from Staines, until one day I found 'my' lamp post distinctly void of bicycle, so I walked the last bit from then on. This probably explains my recurrent dreams of being late for the 8.20 morning meeting, since I was invariably slightly delayed by the train or the walk or both.

Initially Digby slept in a Moses basket in the sitting room. Having no floor space big enough for a cot, we made another of the creative decisions that seem to permeate our liveaboard life. It's not about how much space you have, it's what you do with it that counts. We bought a second hand travel cot on ebay and had some zips put in the sides by the outfitters that later created our cockpit canopy. This meant that the cot could sit on top of one of the double beds, with enough room down the side for one of us to sleep if necessary. Bear in mind that our beds are walled in on three sides already. Although there was practically no room above the cot to the ceiling, the side could be unzipped and the baby posted in that way. It worked for both children until they were able to stand or climb.

I've always thought it a curious philosophy that you need loads of stuff for a newborn. Actually, babies require very little apart from food, love, warmth and your presence. Whilst visiting Mothercare with baby Digby, I was once stopped by a bewildered mother-to-be who was clearly overwhelmed by the array of baby clobber on offer to her. She asked me, as a new mother, what equipment I thought was really essential. I struggled to think and came up with "muslins", which let's face it are quite handy for all sorts (but still not essential, I should have said nappies!). Nonetheless, from the time you announce your pregnancy, there is an immense amount of pressure to acquire all sorts of paraphernalia, and the competitive nature of human beings comes into force.

In most circumstances, comparison is unhelpful. The comparisons that occur quite effortlessly amongst anti-natal groups and at the school gate can complicate your life in limitless ways. You've signed up with an NCT group and you've got nine months in which to complete your perfect birthing plan with accompanying music and poetry. They've encouraged you to check all the boxes indicating your preferences for as natural a birth as possible, gas and air at the very most - and at all costs avoiding any sort of pain medication or, heaven forbid, a Caesarean Section. Pre baby, you're quite certain that you will never be buying anything made of plastic, especially a toy that plays a siren or even a tune when you press its gaudy buttons. Your little one will be an eco-warrior with washable nappies, which of course are really quite economical when you use them again with your second child. Does anybody do that? You abhor the idea of your precious baby's bottom being roughed up with chemical filled baby wipes, which you'll replace with simple cotton wool balls and water; never mind the impracticabilities. You'll pass by those convenient little jars of baby food in the supermarket, preferring to fill your own ice trays with organic mush. You will never, ever, buy your toddler a Happy Meal.

Fuelled with parenting guides such as Gina Ford you deceive yourself for nine whole months. And then; baby arrives. Labour happens. The birthing plan goes out of the window. Motherhood is demanding - and of course very rewarding - and those early days and weeks of getting to know your baby's needs are possibly the most demanding of all. At this stage, you'll sign up for anything whatsoever that you can do to make life that little bit easier. I can smugly admit we did manage washable nappies with Digby for a year, until we went on a French boating holiday, of all things, and had no access to a washing machine, whereupon disposables were, frankly, essential.

When you live on a boat you cannot simply go shopping for recreation. Nothing off the shelf fits. The beds are built in to fit the space, which is shaped by the hull and irregular, and so are the mattresses. You cannot simply acquire a new lamp, a second ladle or a foot spa, however much you desire it. Christmas is dangerous because even if you've understood your limitations in terms of material items, others may not. And it's especially hard when your well-meaning friend or family member has bought something for your children, and you know with a sinking heart you'll have to rehome it, because it simply has no 'home' on the boat. In addition, it's unfair on Thomas to litter the floor with hazards which means a reasonable level of tidiness must be maintained in order to allow him free passage through the boat. There is an invisible 'corridor' maintained through the living space that must not be encroached upon at any cost, although of course it is. The basic rule is, if something comes in, something else goes out. It's a fantastic way to live, not acquiring useless junk all the time. We have minimal storage for clothes and toys so the children have learned to let go of the old to make room for the new - which they do every Christmas and most birthdays. We are healthy suppliers of a wide variety of antiquities to our local Emmaus charity; although this can be a double edged sword as a trip to their warehouse can result in compulsive purchases of seemingly sensible items. It's remarkable how much smaller furniture looks in a warehouse compared to on the boat, not to mention the narrow doorway it has to fit through.

The NCT group in Staines was a big part of our live during that season as we spent a lot of time with them, especially our friend Julie and her sons Gabriel (born 6 days after Digby) and Sebastian (born 3 months before Celeste). We would meet in a playground in Staines or Chertsey in the morning with our Stanley flasks, go home for lunch and naps and invariably meet again in the afternoon, at another playground, each other's houses, the Chertsey bookshop (aka coffee shop) or at the local Notcutts; which had an excellent aquatics department for entertaining toddlers and a reasonable coffee shop for entertaining parents. Notice I mentioned coffee three times in that paragraph. It was an essential part of our well-being in those early sleep deprived days of parenthood. It was Julie who said, 'I don't even know what season it is, never mind what day' - and introduced me to Lavazza.

In 2007 we had another addition to the family; in the form of Thomas's first guide dog, Magic.

Chapter 5: Good and faithful servant

On 24th May 2006, when Digby's arrival was only three months away, a six and a half week old black Labrador X Retriever puppy arrived in Galleywood, Essex, at what was to be his home for nearly a year, and eternal holiday visits. He was the twenty-fourth and last guide dog puppy Gwen and Malcolm took into their home, although they continue to board guide dogs left, right and centre, and cats and budgies besides. Magic lived alongside Gwen and Malcolm's pet Labrador Maisie and a one-year-old flat coated retriever called Morton - who was also destined to be a guide dog, but had developed a real attachment to Malcolm and so, with good luck on his side, made Gwen and Malcolm his permanent home.

So Magic began to learn all he needed to know to prepare him for more formal guide dog training at eleven months old. This included intense socialisation; introducing him to a wide variety of situations such as people, animals, public transport, canal boats, lifts, scaffolding, church communities, hotels, cafes, the beach and toddler groups. Essentially exposing him to all sorts of environments from a very early age so that he would not be fazed when he encountered them on harness later in his working career. He also learned some basic guide dog language such as 'forward', 'stand', 'right' and 'left'. I wonder if little Magic knew that he had landed on all four of his feet in that most loving of homes. We contacted Gwen and Malcolm soon after Magic came to live with us and have kept in touch since. The only place we have left Magic (and his successor Chester) is with Gwen and Malcolm. For Magic it was home from home, whenever we dropped him there we'd get the feeling he was torn whether he wanted to come with us or just stay. His last visit there was with Chester in early August 2019 whilst we were in France, which turned out to be just two weeks before he died peacefully at home on Golden Mean. We are so grateful that he had that special time with Gwen and Malcolm at both the very beginning and the very end of his life.

Dogs were an essential part of my growing up. When my father died, Moss transferred her affections to me, which I welcomed with open arms. Shortly afterwards, we took on another collie, a handsome two year old long coated boy called Ben. Moss surprised us by gaining a new lease of life in the company of the younger dog and we were blessed with her company until she got to the end of the road at the grand age of fifteen years. Ben was a typical high energy collie, he enjoyed the beach and a tennis racket and ball improved the quality of his walk no end. When I passed my driving test (third time lucky) I took him to local shows and obedience classes. He shone in the obedience class; although he was clever enough to realise that he didn't need to perform once out of the village hall where the classes were held and would revert to his wilder side. When travelling in the boot of my first car, an orange Talbot Sunbeam, he would whine all the way home. Sitting next to me on the floor in the passenger foot well, he was happy enough; maybe he didn't take to the idea of being relegated to a second class seat at the back. When I started working in Norwich full time and my mother was away in London much of the time, preparing to move there, it didn't seem fair to Ben to leave him home alone all day. We made the tough decision to rehome him; fortunately finding a local lady who lived with her elderly mother and would offer him continuous company. I still have regrets about letting him go, although I know it was the right one for him with my circumstances fluctuating so much. A couple of years later I moved to London and began a fourteen year stint without a permanent dog in my life – although I borrowed other people's as much as possible.

As my father said in a chapter about dogs in the book he mercifully penned for me only a few years before he died; 'life without a dog is intolerable'. He had grown up with dogs too, but the dog that stole his heart had an extraordinary story. He was walking on the beach one day, whilst training in the Fleet Air Arm at Lee on Solent. He saw some sailors throwing stones in the sea for a collie to chase. He thought it rather cruel that they weren't giving their dog a break or drying him off, as he was now thoroughly wet and bedraggled. As he observed and contemplated interjecting, the sailors left, leaving the dog behind. Philip reacted as any dog lover would; he took the dog home' – which was back to the officers' mess. On making enquiries he located the dog's owner – but he didn't want the dog, and was only too pleased to give him to Philip who would have been in his early twenties at the time. With the wit and humour that made him a great writer, he called the dog 'Digga Rhumby' which is a malapropism for 'Rubber Dinghy'. Digga was adopted as a sort of mascot amongst the officers and often spent time sleeping under the mess officer's desk. He also regularly flew with my father.

When my father was relieved of duty due to the long hours spent in a cramped Spitfire cockpit aggravating an arthritic condition, he and Digga relocated to central London where my father was to set up an advertising partnership. He describes Digga as 'the king of all dogs ' - although of course Moss followed on later and was no less noble in his eyes, in her own way.

Whilst Ben used to take himself on wanders quite frequently, being away for several hours and always returning with no explanation, Moss only once went missing. For ten excruciating days my father could neither paint nor write. His anguish was intense. He or she must have had a guardian angel at work, because the police eventually connected the missing dog report with the older collie that had recently been taken to the dog's home, and reconnected her with my father only a day before she was due to be put down. She had in fact been picked up locally a week before, but in the 80s dogs weren't microchipped, the internet didn't exist, and the authorities were unbearably slow to make the connections. Unbelievably, they only kept older 'stray' dogs for ten days.

Not long after we were married Thomas and I had a frank conversation about dogs. I think I stated something like; "I'd like to get a dog anyway, so it may as well be one that's useful to you." Thomas tells me that navigating with a guide dog, whilst more efficient in some ways, can be a lonelier journey than with a white stick. Not that the dog isn't good company, but Thomas doesn't get to meet and chat to people on the way. Following a route with a guide dog is very much a straight A to B affair, there is no meandering, mooching or spontaneous detours. If friends spot you in town they tend not to make themselves known for fear of disrupting progress. Not dissimilar to the experience of driving Golden Mean into a lock; rather than approach and ask if they can help, gongoozlers scurry to the left and right, like rabbits in the headlights. I once walked behind Thomas working with Magic through Windsor High Street, taking a video clip to send to Gwen and Malcolm to show Magic in his early days of working partnership. I caught on camera the moment a tourist walked out from a shop looking at their phone, not looking where they were walking at all, and collided straight into Thomas and Magic!

London is surprisingly full of people keen to assist. Sometimes too keen. If he was lucky, Thomas and his white stick would be escorted like a baton in a relay race through all the many intersections of his route across London, some even taking a detour to bring him to his destination. Unfortunately there are also people who, whilst meaning well, have absolutely no clue where they are or how they are going to get to their destination. Just as eager to help, they masquerade confidence and lead Thomas down the urban equivalent of the garden path.

On one particular commute across the busy concourse at Victoria Station, Thomas, swiping his white stick left and right and moving swiftly towards the platform, managed to catch the ankles of a tall man sprinting for a train. The man was sent sprawling and, as often is the case when they realise it's a blind person they have bumped into, their auto-response of annoyance at being bumped quickly turns to profuse apology. As Thomas helped him up he apologised for getting in Thomas's way whereupon Thomas recognised the voice and said; "Oh, hello Paul!" The sprawler turned out to be a family friend.

So all things considered, a guide dog seemed like it would be a positive addition to our family in lots of ways and we made some investigations and filled out a detailed form, kick-starting the long process of acquiring a guide dog. This process is akin to an unlikely combination of taking an advanced driving test, a personality analysis for a high powered job and being interviewed with a view to adopt Your suitability continually reassessed at each stage. Home visit include a scrutiny of the general living environment - clearly irregula in our case - and details such as where the dog will sleep. As luck would have it, we had just removed a coal bunker which was located underneath Digby's bed but accessed from the living room. This left a reasonable sized cubby hole, not big enough for a dog to stand but big enough for him to crawl in and lie in his bed with his chin resting on the ledge at the entrance, which was Magic's default pose and the position where he gracefully departed this world.

Magic's trainer was a new recruit in the Guide Dogs organisation and there was little room for flexibility. However she approved of the coal bunker hole, as Magic was apparently a dog who liked to retreat into an enclosed small space, just as some dogs gain security from being in a crate. Magic would be able to get away into his own private area even in such compromised living quarters. Naturally, whenever there were extra people in the boat Magic would choose to stretch out across the entire living room floor rather than retreat to his den. When Chester (Magic's successor) moved in, during the four months he overlapped with Magic we temporarily lost sight of the carpet.

As well as the living space, the surrounding marina environment s under surveillance by the guide dogs team. Since the dog does have o leave the boat to use the toilet, this was a long walk down the pontoon to the area of concrete which would be known as the spending area', which could be hosed down periodically if necessary. t's important that the dog can do its 'business' on command and on any surface as Thomas and Magic might be in central London for the day with no access to a grassy knoll. They talk about potential regular routes that the dog will be doing and assess the potential dog owner's natural walking pace, a curious procedure involving taking the dog handler for a walk on harness. Guide dogs are not granted to all who request them. Having too much sight can cause additional issues as you would be more likely to 'override' the dog. Although it's the handler who needs to memorise the route, the dog has to develop real confidence to make good decisions in ad hoc situations – for example if a van is parked on the pavement or there are roadworks.

Guide dogs are bred in a specific guide dogs' breeding centre in Leamington Spa and, contrary to popular belief, they are not all Labradors. In fact, most are cross breeds, as this is proven to produce a healthier dog with a better temperament. Labrador and Golden Retriever mixes are most common, but there are a few labradoodles with non-shedding coats that won't make your eyes water, but who are generally not as hot at guiding. There are also German Shepherds built for extra stamina, for owners with a higher workload. Thomas's brother has a lovely German Shepherd guide dog called Texan who commutes with William into London most days from Sussex. The Shepherds have the added advantage of making the passage through startled onlookers quite smooth, just by association. Who would mess with a Shepherd in hi-vi?

After nearly two years of waiting, during which time we'd had one child and conceived a second, Thomas was given a small amount of information on Magic; a black Labrador/Retriever cross that was a potential match. Magic came for a visit and hopped into the cockpit, first sitting on Thomas's lap before being told that was not the right way to behave (Thomas, that is. Magic was always in the right).

Magic was known and loved by so many people, having joined us six months before Celeste's birth and being at Thomas's side pretty much every moment until the day after Digby's thirteenth birthday. That day he sat on Thomas's lap in the cockpit for the first time was only the beginning.

The next stage was for Thomas and Magic to attend a twelve day residential training course in a hotel, to get to know each other without distractions (meaning me and baby Digby) and for Thomas to learn how to work the dog on harness. He likens it to learning to drive. It's not relaxing. There is a lot of counting steps, a plethora of code words to learn (For example if you want to turn left at a kerb its called a 'back right', and if you want the dog to pee - or more - you tell it to 'get busy'). On the training course was Amos, a very laid back Israeli who had had a guide dog before, and Shelley and Jim who were both new to guide dogs, like Thomas. The rules were very strict. Digby, now fifteen months, and I were basically not supposed to visit, apart from one day at the weekend. We may have broken the rules slightly. It was quite a big deal, it was the first time Thomas had been away from us and the first time I had been on my own on the boat with the baby. Thomas got to know the other three quite well and there was a fair bit of hanging around waiting for his turn; there being only one trainer for himself, Shelley and Jim.

At the end of the residential you are released to go home. What a happy day that is! But still, no 'free runs' (guide dog speak for a walk in the park) are allowed for two whole weeks. We were simply longing to take a long stroll at Virginia Water or Windsor Great Park with Magic, who was still only nineteen months old. But there is a necessary settling in period, no visitors are allowed and the trainer comes out regularly to begin to learn local routes, which for Thomas included walking to Chertsey about a mile away, and getting on a bus to Staines and walking through to the railway station. Life is planned around the demands of the trainer at this point and it's made clear that this is still very much a probationary period. Gradually things become more routine and the visits from the trainer decrease. This was fortunate as I was becoming increasingly large as I was expecting another baby. We were so concerned that a new baby might be deemed cause to 'take the dog away' (which was regularly suggested as a solution to things not going well) that I made myself absent when the trainer was due to come round. Thomas and Magic had been working together for six months when we had to admit to the trainer that our daughter, Celeste

Rosa Harrison was born, on Golden Mean, on 2nd May 2008. Now we were five on board.

In the same way that Moss only had eyes for my father, Magic quickly formed the same sort of attachment to Thomas. Whilst always friendly, affectionate and bombproof around babies, (and latterly with a variety of small pets running about 'loose in the hoose') Magic's fundamental desire was to be by Thomas's side; whether that be working on harness or at rest. Even at his young age, when Magic first arrived on Golden Mean he already exuded an air of confidence. He was the king of guide dogs. He knew his job and was good at it. He and Thomas spent their early months together navigating a complex route through the back streets of the South bank of London from Waterloo to St James's Park. As I waved goodbye on the station platform at Staines, or when they left for the bus that stopped near the marina, I would entrust Thomas's safety to Magic and offer a prayer for their safe return. Every day was an adventure involving busses, trains, undergrounds and busy London streets, full of what the guide dogs' trainers call 'street furniture'; bins, scaffolding, signage, traffic cones - all sorts of unexpected hazards for Magic to avoid.

When we moved to Norfolk Magic's workload decreased dramatically, as we now live eight miles from the nearest town. Apart from trips to the marina office to collect post, a guide dog is mainly off duty at home until we go into town. Their working life includes lots of short trips, from the car to the rehearsal room, to church, to a shop or to meet a friend in a cafe. Magic enjoyed long country walks and many trips to the beach, visits to friends' houses and holidays to the Peak District and Scotland.

Because of this light workload, Magic was allowed to continue working until he was eleven (guide dogs normally retired at ten). Although he seemed happy to continue to do so, when retirement came and the big day came when the harness was handed back, he did seem to slow down considerably. Most loyal and diligent of dogs, he would have gone on working for Thomas until he dropped. The wait for a successor lasted two years during which time we enjoyed Magic's company in all things as before, simply without the pressure for him to guide. He tolerated Chester's exuberant arrival in March 2019 because that was what he knew was expected of him. We were committed to keeping Magic in his retirement, the thought of him going to live with another family when he was so attached to Thomas didn't feel right at all. We weren't to know then that we had only four months left with Magic. We like to think that during those last months he whispered a few words of advice to Chester, who was still very much learning the ropes and is a very different sort of dog with an even lighter workload - and the inclination to blend in as one of the children.

Magic developed painful joints in later life but was always up for a walk and spent his last day on the beach celebrating Digby's 13th birthday with friends. The end of Magic's life was one of the saddest moments of our family history but also the most peaceful departing we could have wished for him. As Thomas says, Magic was a dog who did things properly in life, and his death was no different. He passed as peacefully into the next world as its possible for a dog to do, in his coal bunker bed with Thomas by his side reassuring him that it was ok to 'go free', which is the guide dog command for the dog to run free when you let it off the lead in the field. We were so blessed that his last moments were at home and without any intervention or tough decisions to make. We scattered his ashes in a nearby churchyard so we can visit him regularly there, especially when we need to consult him on the big decisions in life.

Dear Magic will be remembered and missed by so many. Whatever we did, wherever we went, Magic was there. On Magic's last visit to Gwen and Malcolm, Gwen kindly emailed me with updates. I remember her saying she had been telling Magic what a good dog he was back then, as a puppy, and what a good dog he is now in his old age. He was quite simply, a good and faithful servant to Thomas and a huge blessing in all our lives.

Chapter 6: Education Otherwise

One Spring morning of 2007, I held baby Digby in the 'tiger in the tree' position. That is to say; he was lying tummy down along my forearm with his head by my elbow, as is advised to settle any post-feed tummy troubles with very little babies. As I gently swung my little tiger, I glanced through the porthole down the length of Pontoon N, which separated Golden Mean from the shore by some 50 metres. I have an internal clock that begins to tick when Thomas heads out with his guide dog with the purpose of 'getting busy'; guide dogs lingo for spending a penny - or a sixpence. I am familiar with how long this procedure usually takes and unwittingly withhold a certain amount of tension; until I hear the zips of the cockpit opening and the sound of the dog jumping in, swiftly followed by Thomas.

If it takes longer than my subconscious clock tells me it should, there are two possible eventualities. First and most likely; Thomas has found someone interesting to talk to en route. Second and less optimistically; something has gone wrong; the dog has been distracted and is now leading Thomas in the wrong direction. Depending on how far I let my overactive imagination run riot, I may conclude that they've been run over by a careless driver or fallen into the marina. In parallel with some more endearing characteristics, I have inherited my father' tendency to worry. For someone who was so outwardly calm and solid, my father suffered a surprising amount of internal anguish. Perhaps it is the legacy of war and the memories of the young men he served alongside who didn't come home. When my mother and I went out shopping, leaving him painting in his studio, we'd be certain to be home half an hour before the time we were expected, to save him from imagining all sorts of alarming - if unlikely – possibilities.

As I suspected, Thomas and Magic had paused on their way back from the spending area to chat to our South African neighbour, Jo. With his busy-ness behind him, Magic lay patiently in his fluorescent harness by Thomas's feet on the pontoon. Jo, having been influenced by proxy by the guide dog rulebook, resisted her natural inclination to fondle his velvet ears (Magic's), at least not whilst he was 'working'.

The delightful Brederode family relocated to Chertsey whilst Ray was working in the UK for a few months. On some days, a trip to spend Magic could take forty-five minutes. Being away from South Africa for an extended period meant that Jo was currently home educating their boys Matthew and William, who were about 11 and 9, and for a time I did a little tutoring with Matthew. Digby blessed us a with a long nap in the afternoons until he was 3 years old, so once he was down it would be a quick call through to Jo further down the pontoon - then along Matthew would come with his Maths book. I recall us making up fictional riverside names to fill in the empty box on the front of his workbook labelled 'Name of school:'. It was a pretty relaxed way to do Maths.

When visiting my mother in South Africa in 2011 we had the pleasure of visiting the Brederode family again back in their home in Somerset West, about an hour's drive East along the coast from Cape Town. We reminisced about our time together on the watery world of the Thames, preparing an allotment with manure with our friend Julie, and drinking Jo's favourite - strawberry tea - out of a flask. (Julie's Stanley and ours would have been full of Lavazza, but Jo and her boys enjoyed strawberry tea.)

On the subject of strawberry teas, Jo once brought to Golden Mean the ingredients for a cream tea. I can't remember the occasion but Jo is the sort of person who can make an occasion out of a grey Monday afternoon. She had bought single cream - whether because double or whipping cream was in scant supply or simply in genuine ignorance of quintessentially English tradition I'm not sure - which she gallantly (but unsuccessfully) attempted to whip, before conceding that those particular scones were destined to swim, crowned with a generous helping of strawberry jam, in very runny cream. Like so often when things go just slightly wrong, but not wrong enough to spoil the enjoyment, this simply made the event more memorable. The presence of the Brederode family in our lives in those early days of boat life and parenthood made life more fun. My lasting view of Penton Hook marina was the day we set sail early in the morning bound for Norfolk, on 21st March 2009. Jo, Ray and the boys stood on the end of our pontoon in their pyjamas waving us off; William wearing Jo's Chinese satin slippers. It was the end of that particular era, a happy and formative six years on the Thames on Golden Mean. The adventures of our passage East along the Thames, and subsequently North on the sea, will be documented in the next chapter.

Two years after entering Oulton Broad through Mutford Lock from the North Sea, settled into our new mooring on the River Waveney and having got to know some strangers who would evolve into lifelong friends, we reached the first crossroads in the educational path of our own children. The decision to educate Digby and Celeste outside of school, whilst influencing our subsequent lifestyle enormously, was not in truth a weighty decision. It seemed a natural path to follow given the latitude and longitude of our family thus far.

Eighteen months after losing my father at the age of twelve, I presented regular requests to my mother to allow me to be released from the local comprehensive. After a reasonable first year, I had a growing feeling that it was failing me, in both educational and social respects. After a necessary period of discernment, it became clear to my mother that my unhappiness was not going to pass, and we agreed I would leave school in the October half term of Year 9, to be home educated, which would be achieved via a combination of tutors and correspondence courses. With my own experience and a teaching degree under my belt, the option to home educate Digby and Celeste was always on the cards. In a similar way to the decision to move onto Golden Mean not being the same as the decision to continue living aboard, the initial move to the home education route may not be viewed as a permanent one until it has passed the test of time.

The next crossroads came when Digby approached the age of secondary school entry, and that proved to be a rockier path to negotiate. Whilst Thomas and I were confident we were making the right decision to continue down the home educating path, we were challenged by a few who expressed a genuine concern that we were not. You can get away with being alternative during the primary years, no real harm has been done, but surely now is the time to take their education more seriously? Otherwise..... well, who knows what might happen to them?

When it came to it, the transition from primary to secondary age for Digby was a non event. We just carried on with what we were doing. The main focus, as always, was to ensure that he was progressing. At his own pace. There was no bus to catch. (Or uniform to label). Although I can wax lyrical about the advantages of home education over school, I would be the last person to try and convince anyone that home education is the right path for them or their child In fact, I am quite sure it isn't for the vast majority. Thomas and I are blessed with a rare commodity - time - to enjoy these precious years journeying with Digby and Celeste, we have the ability to work from home and good friends with whom we can lean on for support, and vice versa. We are now unbelievably on the final leg of the journey leading to GCSEs next year. After that, education choices become more independent for Digby and Celeste as they can have greater autonomy in deciding on what sort of further education they would prefer, which will most likely not include us in a teaching capacity, even if we are still essential as a means of transport!

At the time of writing, the world is emerging from an extraordinary year where, due to Covid 19 lockdowns, children across the globe have been learning at home on and off for a year. Home schooling has hit the news. Parents have had no choice other than to get more hands on with their children's learning in 2020, and many have had to juggle an impossible home/work balance. But there are distinct differences with those who have made the active choice to educate their children away from school because of the long term benefits. Doubtless there will be a few who have decided, having dipped their toes in the water, that this is a path they would now like to follow. But I can hear an audible sigh of relief from the vast majority of both parents and children as the schools prepare to reopen their doors.

One of the pros of educating outside school is the enormous freedom as to how we organise our week. Our days rarely follow the same pattern. We live on the river where Broadland and arable fields meet, and there is an infinite opportunity to learn right on our doorstep, just by actively engaging in the gift of God's creation. During good weather we spend more time outdoors. If a friend or grandparent happens to be visiting, we down sticks with the formal bookwork and take advantage of their company. Perhaps surprisingly, there is no legal obligation to follow the National Curriculum in terms of either teaching plans or tests. We have chosen to work towards taking GCSEs in the core subjects, solely for the purpose of not shutting any doors to further education.

Digby and Celeste have never attended school, although they've spent plenty of time in school buildings with us participating in the musical theatre groups that we used to run full time as after-school clubs. They have thus far had no inclination to be educated in a school and their alternative lifestyle is perfectly normal to them. Any child who has spent significant time in school prior to being home educated will surely tell you that de-schooling takes time to adjust to. It's hard to shake off the habitual timetables and the constantly repeating mantra that learning takes place between 9-3.30, Monday to Friday. To escape the unspoken principle that if you aren't sitting at a desk studying books, then you aren't really learning properly, that holidays are a setback, that play is only beneficial to primary age pupils and that if you don't test regularly then you'll fall behind. And the big one; that you need to attend school in order to form proper friendships, learn how to deal with bullies and basically avoid introversion and isolation. No wonder society can't wait for lockdown to end; lockdown home schooling is home education with none of the benefits!

Our view is that every situation is an opportunity to learn, whether it be formal or informal. As the children have grown older they have become more engaged with current affairs, religion and politics and enjoy discussing these topics with us and with others. Although they have been home educated all their life, much of what they have learned over the years did not take place at home.   Since before they could walk and talk they have been welcome participants in events which would normally be considered inappropriate for children; weddings, funerals, discussion groups, the local hustings, community events and volunteering alongside us with our learning disabled adult drama group - as well as travelling, often during term time. When I was fourteen and not long out of school, my mother and I spent three months of the Winter visiting my Aunt in Mexico, which was rich in culture and full of educational potential; but which might not fit neatly into the National Curriculum.

What are the greatest gifts Thomas and I can offer our children as they begin their metamorphosis into young adults, in this fast changing world of ours? We prioritise spending time together as a family in these golden days while they are still living at home. We take their emotional and educational needs seriously, in that order. We strive to nurture a sense of security and self-worth that will remain with them throughout the storms of life. We have gathered around us an eclectic mix of friends and family who actively participate in our children's lives and help them to better understand and express themselves. We have chosen to prioritise Christian values over worldly ones and continually seek out others who can mentor and inspire our children in their faith. We encourage an interest in social, moral and philosophical matters and hope that they will have the strength to make their voices heard in the cacophony of society where resolve can so often be weakened by peer pressure and institutional conditioning. We model a creative approach to life and encourage them to think unconventionally - surely a vital skill as they navigate any choppy waters ahead.

It is our sincere hope that Digby and Celeste can draw on some of the more unusual experiences and environments we have immersed them in, not least their unusual home, as they go forth boldly and embrace whatever their adult futures may hold.

Chapter 7: Time and Tide: Golden Mean's Great Voyage

Around the middle of February every year, I begin to stare long and hard at the willow trees that enclose the marina, waiting for a bubble of green to appear on their long slender branches. In my mind's eye the buds emerge and the branches are miraculously transformed from bare woolly trailers into a cascading green fountain. In reality this transfiguration does not take place until March gallops in, on whose back ride snowdrops, daffodils, longer evenings and a distinct feeling of relief in the air. It's not only the boating community that are emerging from their Winter hibernation with renewed zest for life, after what has been a long and, dare I say it, particularly cold and damp Winter. On New Year's Eve we moved our boat to the only working tap on the marina and filled up our tanks with fresh water. By Epiphany we were thoroughly iced in as not only the pipes were frozen but also the marina itself.

Despite the water shortage we enjoyed long wood fire evenings and toasted teacakes, the company of friends, family and hot chocolate. With the surge of energy that the Spring brings, comes our decision to move to waterways new. To the casual observer this might seem like an irrational and somewhat spontaneous reaction to the long Winter, but the close friends who know us well astutely acknowledged that 'they saw it coming'. One too many trips to Norfolk to visit old haunts and a few Winter evenings online, and the Norfolk Broads has become the object of our desire. I long for the wide open skies and far away horizons of my childhood home. Most of the coast is designated an 'area of outstanding natural beauty' and there is a beach for every mood. You can canter along a wide sandy beach (on or off a horse), skim pebbles into rough seas, and eat ice-cream on the quay watching the sun set over the marshes listening to the sound of oystercatchers and the tinkling halyards of the dinghies on the hard. Where old friends welcome us warmly for cups of tea and homemade cake. For the quiet, black muddy earth, the cold crisp days, getting stuck behind a tractor and it not mattering. For a bulge of the British Isles that has less than average rainfall and is virtually an island; where change comes slowly and the locals go back centuries and are proud of their county, where 'the city' is Norwich and London is only just near enough for a day trip.

In January 2009 we stayed in Robin's daughter's holiday house and spend two days driving down to South Norfolk to visit some barely open marinas, finally securing a mooring on the River Waveney. Our rationale: if the location seemed in any way inviting in the Winter months that it could only improve in the Summer. In the weeks that followed, family and friends have been cajoled, bribed and cooked into submission, lending their support with battening TVs and fridges as well as hatches, fitting a new bathroom, signage, paintwork and the like. Our skippers have been arm-twisted and float in wait on their own boats at Chelsea Harbour, promising safe passage, electronic charts, handheld plotters and bags of experience.

Lest it appear that the decision to move our home and our world be an easy one to make, let me counter all the aforementioned temptations. In the five and a half years we have called the Thames our permanent anchorage, we have had a wedding, two amazing children and acquired a very special black Magic. As our lives became more centred around home and the commutes into London became less frequent, we began to develop some special friendships in our community. We (almost) planted an allotment and drank copious amounts of Lavazza out of flasks in just about every playground in the Spelthorne area. We adopted a South African family on another boat, fired homemade rockets over the aforementioned willow trees and did maths and handwriting practice in the 'River's End' School at the end of the pontoon. We walked the towpaths and Savill Gardens, collected leaves, feathers and stones and made collages out of them. We spent Port's 2nd birthday at a ploughing match with the toddlers in seventh heaven and the babies looking on. We gained two very special little boys as godsons who we hope will continue to be part of our lives and adventures. The Thames valley has been kind to us, but now it's time for this crew to be Swallows and Amazons for a while. No doubt I'll be scrutinizing the willows for buds in the Waveney Valley next Spring but first we have an epic voyage to undertake.

The time has come to say goodbye

With preparations for what we now call 'The Great Voyage' going on a pace, there was limited opportunity to reflect on what it will be like to say goodbye to what we have called home for nearly six years. It was the river that brought us here and the river will be the path we leave by. We knew no-one when we came but have made valued friendships, which will continue wherever we should drop anchor. On the day that we cast off our mooring lines at the marina it really will be the end of an era. When we enter the tidal Thames it will be the start of a new one. The familiar staff at Waterloo station that know I wish to catch the Reading train, and fast track us through when running late, will be a thing of the past. The bus drivers that know we want to alight outside Gate 2 of the marina might wonder as they pass what happened to that bloke with the guide dog. The seagull that sits on the top of our mast will be disappointed to lose the highest vantage point over the marina. Sandi in the kebab shop, Elaine at the Vet's, John the Butcher and Maria the hairdresser will all be bade farewell, along with the familiar Chertsey life they represent.

As a guide dog user I know the pavements on our routes in intimate detail, but know that as time passes those memories will fade, like old student flat telephone numbers. Some memories will remain with me forever. Cliveden where we were married is still the nicest stretch of the river and perhaps one day Celeste will ask me questions like 'Where was I born?' and 'Where did you have your wedding reception?' Both will require us getting into a dinghy to give a full explanation. We have history here, but the time has come to say goodbye. Norfolk will be a new chapter with all sorts of challenges for us. The first, of course is to get there.

Thomas, early March 2009

* * *

If you look closely through the muddy wet hair, you might just notice the squarish bronze tag affirming that this Labrador, caked in the finest mud that Savill Gardens has to offer, has an alter-ego as a working guide dog. Not just any old guide dog; but a nautical guide dog. Perhaps the only one of his kind? The messy romp near Windsor Great Park is a last fling with his owner, to whom he is devoted, before they must part for a week or two, whilst the young guide dog's floating home is relocated to the Norfolk Broads. Unaware that he has walked his last walk along Pontoon N - a walk he has done hundreds of times since moving aboard eighteen months ago - he is now heading to the place he called home for the first year of his life and where he will waste no time climbing into his doggy friend Morton's bed and take advantage of the company of his most favourite human friends; Gwen and Malcolm. He won't miss rocking around on the North Sea, nor will he miss having to be ferried by dinghy to the shore whilst moored on a buoy at Queenborough on the south side of the Thames estuary. He will be greatly missed by the crew, who will have to clean up their own crumbs, but he will soon be reunited and happily swop the London Underground escalators and tube trains for sleepy Beccles pavements and endless open fields.

The crew of the Golden Mean are up early; their skippers Paul and Max arrive before breakfast and are keen to cast off. There is a somewhat frantic rush to say goodbye to great friends and neighbours, some of whom are still asleep on this otherwise lazy Saturday morning. Those that are up and about hug the crew tight at the end of Pontoon N. To a casual observer, this might seem like just another cruise for Golden Mean, leaving her mooring for a few hours or days was a regular occurrence, returning a few days or weeks later after visiting Windsor, Cookham or Shepperton. But the tearful pyjama-clad friends know that this time Golden Mean and her crew - romantically dubbed The Captain, No.1, Port and Starboard for this Great Voyage - will not be returning, perhaps ever, to this particular stretch of the Thames

Goodbyes are never easy, but without an ending there can be no beginning.

As if giving her own blessing, the sun beams down on the crew, who comprise a couple in their thirties with their eleven month old baby and her toddler brother, two skipper friends they have acquired for the voyage; and the paternal grandmother who has joined them for the Thames portion of the voyage. After the early morning frost, the day is unseasonably warm, for which they are grateful. With Golden Mean's cockpit canopy removed for better visibility and her mast lowered out of reverence for the many bridges she would pass beneath, the steel sailing barge cuts a sleek path through the water. Her destination; Chelsea Harbour - her first overnight stop on the Great Voyage to Norfolk. Around teatime she will alight on the same pier that the Queen will later use to board the vessel that would convey her down the same river in a flotilla to mark her Diamond Jubilee in 2012.

Taking it in turns to steer, work locks and make tea, the crew have no need for stoppages, were it not for the unforeseen clash of dates with the Heads of the River boat race. With the river unexpectedly closed to all other boating traffic downstream of Kew Bridge, the crew makes the most of the opportunity to turn off the engines and relax for an hour or so over lunch, moored alongside a houseboat called the Queen Elizabeth. Four pedestrians wave down from their vantage point on top of Kew Bridge, and would no doubt come aboard - were access to Golden Mean easier. They are not strangers, but the Captain's father in law and his friends, who have followed Golden Mean's progress from Penton Hook, but with her galley (and crew) inaccessible they will doubtless continue to a leisurely pub lunch somewhere on the riverbank.

At Teddington Lock, Starboard's godparents eagerly await the arrival of Golden Mean. Not able to come aboard - due to Port and Starboard currently being stricken with chicken pox, coinciding with Danielle being pregnant with their son - the crew are nonetheless able to offload a jetwash that they had loaned the crew in preparation for the Great Voyage.

Now in tidal waters, Golden Mean approaches Putney Bridge and the King's Head where the Captain had spent many an evening off-duty with her Samaritan colleagues, who had become her close friends. One of these friends, a slight figure in a turquoise scarf, now dashes along the riverbank, weaving through surprised bystanders and occasionally stopping to photograph Golden Mean as her black hull glides through the water, her red stripe flashing in the sunlight. Still more friends with cameras, downstream of the bridge, leaping up and down, waving and shouting. The crew squint, trying to distinguish their cheerleaders amidst the merry revellers leftover from the boat race Once sighted they are acknowledged with copious horn blowing from

No.1 who is sitting on the bow with the Captain. Port and Starboard sleep on in their cabin. Just another day on the river.

Battersea Bridge and Chelsea loom with high rises all around, incongruously urbane and still, flanking the constantly moving river with its plethora of craft of every size and purpose. Golden Mean fits snugly on the inside of the pier, which is situated on the outside of the harbour. There is another much bigger barge on the outside of the pier. A single liveaboard, Charmaine, who is relocating to a mooring at Gravesend. Another voyage, another story. I wonder if she remembers the crew of the Golden Mean? Chelsea will be the crew's home for another two weeks, although they don't know it yet as they hope to continue their journey tomorrow. Time and tide wait for no man - and the weather doesn't succumb to the will of the people. After dark, Port admires the twinkling lights that ascend from the shoreline high into the sky, and by day he watches the swarm of helicopters using Battersea Heliport; like bees around a honeypot.

Mother's Day dawns at Chelsea with clear blue skies and the neighbour is planting her roof garden. The Captain is making Port a bacon butty and is reminded of her childhood in North Norfolk and getting up early to eat breakfast at anchor in Blakeney harbour. Port is standing in the middle of the living room floor feeling the movement and watching the glass boats on his dangling mobile sway like he hasn't seen before. The Captain has noticed both children catching the view of the sky risers through the portholes with a somewhat surprised look on their faces - their view has changed dramatically overnight!

No.1 dangles over the bow, fighting valiantly with the bowsprit, trying not to drop tools and fittings into the depths. The tide is coming in again. With the extra hands of Charmaine to assist, he is able to shoot the pin in at just the right moment and emerges from the battle triumphant. Golden Mean is now about twelve feet longer. He then has to launch the dinghy to attach the lower cable. Not easy when you're trying to hold yourself in place with one hand and the tide is trying to push you the other way. The drum is fixed on at the end of the bowsprit so the furling head sail can be attached later.

Golden Mean waits for the right weather to depart. It won't be today. There is a strong Westerly breeze which is forecast to reach Force 7 later on. Far too windy for The Great Voyage, despite blowing in the right direction. Today she is rolling round a lot, to the point where things are starting to roll off worktops. The little children are just about managing to remain upright. Good preparation for the sea voyage. The coming days promise north westerlies, which might work for the Thames passage, but would offer a very choppy passage north, after Golden Mean has turned left out of the estuary into the North Sea. Patience will have to trump frustration, until the wind backs round to the South West. Paul and Max, who skippered Golden Mean from Penton Hook to Chelsea, have suggested Burnham on Crouch as the first stop on the journey north. Golden Mean first floated on the Crouch for her sea trials in 1995 when she was brought down on a trailer with a police escort from Lancashire where she was built. Port and Starboard's Uncle William promises to pop in after work tonight - there is a river taxi that will bring him along from Blackfriars Bridge right to their very pier. The Captain noticed some suited bods wandering down the ramp this morning and wondered where they were heading, then discovered the water taxi service.

Out at sea, there is a Gale Force 8 imminent, meaning 3-4 metre waves. Golden Mean will move reluctantly into the inner harbour tomorrow, envious of the Dutch Barge next door who departs for her new mooring at Gravesend accompanied by a flying escort; the greylag goose who has laid some eggs on her deck. A variety of visitors - both good friends and more distant acquaintances - will drop by over the coming two weeks, whilst Golden Mean languishes trapped in the confines of the trendy Chelsea harbour basin, surrounded by empty high rise flats. The atmosphere in the basin is quite different from the river; it's quiet, verging on eerie. The other boats unoccupied, Golden Mean flanked by enormous sea going cruisers going nowhere. The Captain ransacks the cupboards for white wine and peanuts to entertain the steady trickle of uninvited guests, being as welcoming as she can muster.

The Captain is impressed. No.1 has been working very hard. Singlehandedly, in the dark, he has retrieved a spaghetti junction of halyards from where they were stowed under the bed in the front cabin. He has detected which rope belongs to which pulley, threading them through on the mast which is still horizontal. Despite the jumble of ropes in the cockpit, which is most definitely no longer a play area, he has made order out of chaos. After a hailstorm and countless cups of tea, and with help from friends David and Andy, the mast goes up and the ropes miraculously all seem to be doing what they were intended to do. Golden Mean fully dressed includes all three sails. A magnificent sight - but Chelsea Harbour is devoid of interest. Not a gongoozler in sight. Not a soul comes to watch.

Golden Mean is ready and waiting, but it gradually dawns on her crew that their skippers are not. After the two week weather delay, they now have other business to attend to. The crew of Golden Mean must find someone else to help. All friends with sailing experience are contacted - and all decline the responsibility of skippering Golden Mean on the high seas. In desperation, the Captain follows an improbable lead. Joe, whom she has never met but has been conversing with online during the past few weeks of voyage preparation, sails a traditional wooden Norfolk Broads yacht. She guesses, from their electronic conversations, he is in his fifties or sixties a salty Norfolk sea dog with much local knowledge. Joe guesses that the skipper of this large barge ('Hilly Harrison') is male and offers to buy him a pint when at last Golden Mean reaches Norfolk. She gracefully accepts the offer, whilst gently informing him of his error. Age and gender aside, the vital detail is that Joe and his friend Chris have agreed to skipper Golden Mean to Norfolk. They will come to London from Norwich by train, at just two days notice. The crew of Golden Mean are eternally grateful for these total strangers who, despite the youngest crew members both recovering from chicken pox (which Joe may or may not have had, he can't remember) will be arriving on Saturday morning ready to skipper Golden Mean and its little family North. They have been treading water for two long weeks and are itching to get out of the harbour, into the North Sea and on up to their mooring in Norfolk.

Another pier, another family, another goodbye. As Golden Mean is released from the harbour and once again moored to the pier, ready for departure, her new skipper strides across the marina with charts in his hand and a coat made from an old sail. Far from a salty sea dog, he is a mere twenty-three years of age. Despite the lack of weathered furrows, he takes things seriously for a young man. He has been on the river all his life. His friend Chris, ten years older, is cheerful and friendly and quickly dubs Starboard 'small fry'. Soon the goodbyes will be underway and Chelsea Harbour will fade into the distance and eventually disappear from view. The Great Voyage is underway.

Again the banks of the Thames are lined with cheerleaders. Big Ben appears first in Port's bedroom porthole then swiftly moves to the sitting room and the galley. It is both extraordinary and every day at the same time. Golden Mean is captured through the lens of Uncle Dom's video camera from the Dome, and the moment immortalised to music as Golden Mean is overtaken by a hovercraft with Auntie Clare shouting to the crew who have no hope of hearing her so far away. Grandmajo's voice waivers as she phones through to the crew from a succession of piers on the South Bank, as Golden Mean is silhouetted against the sunset. After the Thames Barrier, the mast goes up. Next it's the QE2 bridge which appears, towers above them, and disappears. It is Uncle Stuart who takes the iconic photo from the North Bank with Golden Mean barely noticeable under the span of the great suspension bridge. Now there is some serious looking traffic on the river and Golden Mean, who once looked large on the river near Staines, is diminished by the ferries and cargo vessels that occupy the busy Thames Estuary. This is no place for joy riders, but she can hold her own. Shortly after six thirty, a floating mooring is secured at Queenborough; Golden Mean is safely at anchor for the night. The skippers waste no time leaping into the dinghy and head for the local public house, handing over their lifejackets and oars to Grandmajo and Grandpa on the slipway who have caught up by car and row over to join the crew for supper and tales of the Thames. A couple of hours later, this action is repeated in reverse, and Joe and Chris spend their first night on board.

Day Two of The Great Voyage and once through the narrow 'West Swin' channel, it's time for Golden Mean to assume her full character. One mast and three sails; the huge tan mainsail blotting the clouds with the wooden gaff making it tower over the red flag atop the mast. The smaller tan staysail in front of the main, and the white furling headsail which is unrolled from the drum on the end of the bowsprit, completes her attire. Engine off. Golden Mean ceases to purr and now she glides, smoothly and silently, through the gentle waves. The relief from the engine noise is palpable. In the perfect conditions the rigging is tried and tested and the crew are able to converse at normal volume and even Skype Granny Partridge in South Africa and introduce her to the Skipper. The Captain is sure she saw a porpoise. A moment in time.

* * *

'Gold 'n' Mean'

It was one of those days when you wouldn't be anywhere else. The sun was shining and the engines were off. Golden Mean's sails were all out and we were making moderate progress in the gentle breeze. She's a completely different boat under sail, shouldering over at a sedate angle, the rhythmic slosh of water around her bows. It was a golden few hours, but everything would change, oh so rapidly, and we would call upon a very different side to her character. We'd been enjoying the sailing but the breeze was light and our average speed of five knots was dropping off; edging us towards an arrival in Shotley after dark, which we were keen to avoid.

We motored on and about an hour out of port our helm noticed it for the first time; a huge wall of fog rolling in from the open sea. Two sailing boats were away on the horizon and the further one simply vanished. The second was consumed just a few minutes later demonstrating the speed fog can move. Without radar of our own and approaching Harwich and Felixstowe; the busiest container ports in the UK, we did not want to be caught out in the fog any longer than we could possibly avoid. Speed was increased and I went below deck to look after Starboard. Her blue eyes sparkled, unaware of the approaching danger. At that exact moment I heard the command to go to maximum power.

Golden Mean's twin 4.1 Litre engines bellowed and the response was dramatic. Like a lioness protecting her cubs she gave it all she'd got. "Get them home, get them in, get them safe," she roared. The North Sea streamed by at twelve hundred feet per minute. One hundred and forty thousand watts of raw power churned the water below erupting in a boiling tumult several metres astern. Our navigator made swift calculations changing our final destination from Shotley Gate to the lifeboat pier at Harwich. We rocketed towards the harbour. Every second counted now. The white curtain rapidly approached - but so did our destination. Then, suddenly we were engulfed. Visibility was down to fifty feet and we eased back on both engines. Some very careful navigation was called for now and, as if by magic, each marker buoy came out of the gloom like clockwork. Our helm knew the layout of the harbour as mercifully he worked in the town. This proved invaluable. With tremendous skill and taking regular GPS readings as our course converged with other shipping lanes we arrived and moored behind the pier where he often eats his sandwiches. Just 15 minutes later we saw the huge hull of the P and O ferry slip by as she too entered the harbour. Hoorah for Joe and Chris and hoorah for Golden Mean! Most days she's golden, but that night she was definitely mean.

Thomas Harrison, 5th April 2009

* * *

As the crew breathe deep sighs of relief, the skippers escape to the pub. No dinghy required tonight, and Chris has local knowledge (not just about the harbour). Port and Starboard are unaware of the drama of the day; they just want supper.

Dawn breaks on the third day. The crew are excited as they will soon reach their final destination. Or as final as any destination can be, when you live aboard. Their future is not yet known, but this new mooring will still be home some twelve years later when Port and Starboard are entering the teenage years and the Captain is cajoled into writing about their adventures. On their left is Pakefield, and they pass by what will become a familiar beach where memories will be captured for years to come. Land is barely in sight as it's cloudy and they are still several miles off shore. During the subsequent decade, they will celebrate birthdays on the beach, swim in the sea and make tea in their friend's beach hut, looking out to the channel markers and reminiscing about the day that they 'came past here in Golden Mean'.

After a less dramatic passage than the previous day, they approach the harbour under engines and calls are made to the lifting road bridge and the lock. It's Monday afternoon at 4pm. Later they will realise that this was the worst possible time for the Harbour Bridge to lift, with its end of the day traffic queues piling up. Today they are oblivious, thinking only of their arrival at the Waveney River Centre As they approach the lock, Joe, for the first time since departing from Chelsea, relinquishes control of Golden Mean to the Captain. After all he reasons: "You've had more experience in locks than me." How can she refuse? So the Captain assumes a familiar position on the helm and brings them safely through the lock, the last lock they will enter for at least twelve years.

Leaving the lock behind and entering Oulton Broad, the water expands; it's wide and pretty flanked by expensive houses on one side and the Nicholas Everitt park on the other, more unknowns that will become old friends. The Broad will become the place of tea at anchor, swimming with friends, sailing dinghies and playing at the park. Twenty minutes later and St Mary's Church comes into sight with its' Ziggurat tower and thatched roof that burnt down more than once. Grandmajo has come ahead in the red van and is standing on the shoreline with her camera, waiting. At first all she can see is the top of the Douglas Fir mast, towering above the tan reed bank, for it is still early April and the reeds haven't yet grown their Summer plumage. The crew have the marina in sight now, and No.1 holds Starboard swathed in a blue blanket, for evening approaches on the river and it's getting chilly. Her face and fingers are covered in chocolate.

Mummy has been busy at the helm for an hour or so, and Starboard is getting restless. Daddy has opened a box of chocolate fingers to distract her from the end of a journey that she is more than ready to complete. Port is still playing with his magnetic Thomas the Tank Engine down below deck. Mummy will bring in Golden Mean to the marina in a moment, reversing into their new mooring like a local.

Their memories of this journey will form when they are older, from the stories they hear their parents tell of the Great Voyage, the photos that were taken and the book that has yet to be written. But whether or not they know it now; they are home.

Chapter 8: Noah's Ark

As I draw near the end of these chapters, it is twelve years to the day since I reversed into our Norfolk mooring for the very first time at the culmination of our three day sea voyage. I have completed the same manoeuvre many times since, but never have I become complacent about the process. It's almost worth taking Golden Mean out on the river simply for the feeling of relief when we are safely moored up and the engines go off. If conditions are good - meaning that it's not so windy that it will blow us sideways, and the tide isn't so low that we might get stuck in the middle of the marina whilst reversing - it usually goes well. Practise makes practically perfect. And I avoid going out in high winds. When it goes badly; you can be fairly certain there will be gongoozlers. When it goes perfectly, there's a slight disappointment that nobody was watching.

The marina where we live is situated on the Norfolk side of the river from Carlton Marshes, which has been recently redeveloped by the Suffolk Wildlife Trust. We enjoy the sights and sounds of all sorts of wildlife from migrating geese to oystercatchers, marsh harriers, heron, egrets, cormorants and kingfishers. Dawn and dusk provide a cacophony of bird noise as a backdrop to our lives. We have a visiting seal who seems to cruise the inland waterways solo, and turns up every now and again. Otters are plentiful and can be heard playing and crunching fish under the hull. It's a delightful place to live, close to nature.

Having grown up with the two collies, a succession of cats, a multitude of guinea pigs and rabbits, and in teenage years a donkey joined by a succession of borrowed horses; the size of our floating home has not curbed my desire to fill our lives with small creatures. After settling in Norfolk, the pet to person ratio began to increase. Fuelled by me, aided and abetted by our two children and gracefully accepted by Thomas who - despite all the sensible reasons to resist - loves them all as much as we do. In 2019, after Magic had been retired for two years, but was still living with us enjoying his senior years off duty, Thomas acquired his second guide dog, Chester. Another twelve days residential training, this time in Norwich, where we were once again banished from visits; with the exception of a small window of opportunity on Mother's Day when we were allowed to join Thomas and Chester for lunch at the hotel. Chester, another black Labrador / Retriever cross, had big paws to fill. A slightly bigger, much livelier and infinitely more puppy-like dog than Magic - he has nonetheless matured into a helpful working dog and when off duty is a playful family pet.

My donkey, Oscar, whom I acquired when I was fifteen, had been taken in by a friend's mother when I moved from North Norfolk to London in 1993. On making contact some years later, I discovered that

Oscar was still alive and well, and whilst revisiting Norfolk on holidays, prior to moving here permanently, we began to pop in to see him. There is something quite extraordinary about introducing your childhood pet to your own children, and I am grateful for the connection as they now remember him as I do. Once living in Norfolk again full time we were able to visit him at the Arnolds' farm regularly. If I didn't live on a boat, I suspect I'd live on a smallholding of some sort and take on all sorts of extra animals and maybe children too. Just as living on a boat implies a strictly practical relationship with material goods, so it also curbs the temptation to grow one's family too big - both children and animals. But not entirely. We have been dubbed 'Noah's Ark' on more than one occasion.

The small pets began with a couple of guinea pigs; Smartie and Badger, who lived inside the boat, in a cage that fitted snugly into a cubby hole to the right of the stairs as you come down into the cabin. Opposite our little fridge which sits in the cubby hole on the left. Living in close proximity with any animal encourages a different relationship than with one that lives outdoors. You can really get to know and bond with them, and they become relaxed and easily handle-able. Smartie and Badger enjoyed the tail end of the vegetable matter of our meals for many years, to the extent that they knew the sound of the knife on the chopping board and would come to the front of the cage expectantly. In latter years a couple of baby Lionhead lop-eared rabbits were brought home (by me) as an Easter surprise. An impractical

117

impulse decision, diverting my attentions from the already growing desire for a puppy. They needed more space than the guinea pigs, so after a spell inside where they were let loose on the floor regularly, they now live outside on the grass in a large run - although they have to retreat to the upper deck of their hutch periodically when a particularly high flood tide covers the grass.

Some years back we 'rescued' a lone duckling that was under attack from a swan. We named him Sixto having just enjoyed the documentary Searching for Sugar Man, the story of the Mexican musician Sixto Rodrigues. Sadly Sixto the duckling only survived for two weeks - but in those two weeks formed a huge dependency on us (and us on him) and literally came everywhere with us in a box. Ducklings imprint on their 'parents' and don't do well in isolation. Waves of tears were shed when he departed this world. But hearts are made to be broken, and this became the beginning of our love affair with ducks. Next came the four Khaki Campbell ducklings which we purchased a few days old and nurtured until they were old enough to be released into the marina. In subsequent years we purchased an incubator and traversed the Norfolk and Suffolk countryside, picking up an eclectic mix of 'hatching eggs'.

The miraculous process of an ordinary looking egg sitting apparently dormant in an incubator for 28 days and then bursting forth into a fluffy duckling – arguably one of the most adorable creatures or this planet - is one that I think everyone should experience, at least once. The period from when the chick first pips a crack in the shell, to the duckling actually hatching, can take a day or two. Some don't make it. Opinions on whether or not one should intervene with midwifery skills are equally strong in both camps. Having seen some chicks struggle and not make it, I usually feel compelled to at least try, but it's a tense operation which is not always successful. Over a few Summers, we hatched Aylesbury, Indian Runner and any other variety we could get hold of. We kept them inside in the cubbyhole that the guinea pigs used to occupy, for about two weeks until we could no longer keep up with the amount of mess they produced. They were named, handled, ran free on the floor, cuddled on the sofa and introduced to friends. Magic was incredibly tolerant. They were then moved outside into what is now the rabbit run until they were fairly covered in adult feathers and had a good chance of survival in the wild world.

Our friend and neighbour Ashley helped us create a floating duck raft made of an old desk of his son's and a rabbit hutch, which was floated just behind Golden Mean for the ducks to overnight in to help keep them safe from predators. One of our Runner ducks was tufted, crowned with what looked like a pompom, much to the amusement of the holiday visitors, who must have thought they had come to some sort of exotic safari park. Another young Runner got trapped under the boardwalk, and one of the campers, having heard her cries, helped release and reunite her with us - after requesting to borrow our claw hammer. Another runner was born with a deformed curved neck and Celeste learned to lovingly position him over the food and water at regular intervals. An Aylesbury that we purchased from a local farm to enlarge our flock (we like to say rescued, since she was destined for the table), started laying her own eggs – one a day - in random places around the marina. We collected, incubated and hatched a really mixed bag of ducklings, given that she had become quite friendly with all the native (or not so native) breeds of ducks on the marina.

Sadly, there are many natural predators for a free range duck, and especially one that cannot fly like an Aylesbury or a Runner. Our hearts were broken again and again as each day one of our feathered friends would not appear for breakfast. The Khaki Campbells, as flying ducks, had the best survival rate, one of them was around for many years with his mallard friends, only quite recently did we stop seeing him. We hang on to the hope that they've simply moved on to a more appealing habitat, across the river on Carlton Marshes, perhaps.

After the ducks came quail. We first hatched Japanese quail, which are the sort that lay your fancy speckled eggs that cost a fortune in the farm shop. Just last year we surprised Celeste with some hatching eggs for her 12th birthday, and hatched Chinese quail, which are smaller and prettier with all sorts of colours. We also hatched four white pheasants, which appeared to be inherently unhealthy. One of them survived a whole month, and she was named Peacock, and lived with the rabbits when she was bigger. The quail produce tiny eggs the size of a Cadburys mini-egg, which are quirky, colourful and delicious. Hatching is an addictive process and a clear example of the miracle of God's creation. The quail hatch very quickly, we describe it as being like popcorn popping. Blink and you miss it. They are a similar size and texture to a bumblebee.

Digby would love a parrot. This request, like the one for a pet snake, is answered with the standard answer that Thomas and I have used to answer requests over the years, when the answer could be a straight 'no': the gentler response; "When you get your own boat." A parrot would be a more logical bird to keep on a boat. We did once have a bird that would sit on our shoulder. Perhaps the most unusual house guest in our ark was Apollo the pigeon. Found under the willow tree, fluffy and too young to fly or feed himself, it appeared that he had been attacked either in or out of the nest, perhaps falling out when under attack from a crow. Nevertheless, his wounds healed themselves and for a few weeks he lived inside with us, sitting on a shelf by the sofa. I thought that the ducks were messy, but feeding a young pigeon is hard core. You have to make a mush and literally force it down their throat, requiring two people (ideally wearing full PPE), one to hold his beak open and the other to shoot in the mush, using a plastic syringe. Several times a day. Celeste was brilliant at it. The mush went everywhere, but Apollo thrived and eventually learned to fly. One day he flew from the open cockpit to our neighbour's boat and back again.

The next day we went out, leaving the door open, and when we returned he was gone. Needless to say, we believe that one of the many pigeons that alight here regularly is likely to be our Apollo.

This story began with a collie, and it's going to end with one too. I could never quite shake the collie thing out of my system. Some people get to their forties and fifties and have an obsessional longing for a Porsche, a motorbike, a holiday house in the country, or a conservatory. Call it a midlife crisis, empty nest syndrome (not yet in my case) or the change of life - it is what it is.

A couple of years ago I undertook to read the Bible from cover to cover. During the early books of the Bible the character of Moses really caught my sympathies. Moses has a tough job. A job he doesn't want to take on. He feels inadequate for what is being asked of him, and yet God doesn't give him the option to say no. With deep humility and complete faith in his Creator God he leads the exodus out of Egypt, wanders about in the desert with some frankly rebellious and stroppy Israelites, who watch him perform miracle after miracle with God's power and yet; their default position is still to do their own thing. Eventually, after years in the wilderness they reach the promised land, which God shows to Moses from a mountaintop (a reoccurring theme) whilst telling him that, due to one teeny slip up years ago back at Meribah, that Moses himself, will never enter the promised land. It'll be Joshua, not Moses that gets the milk and honey reward. It's a gripping story, well worth a read. Moses has to be my favourite old testament character, and there are plenty to choose from. I thought at the time, "When I get my next collie, I'll call him Moses". That was that.

Finding the right dog, when you've got a clear image of what you want in mind, is almost as difficult as waiting for the right guide dog to be matched to its new owner. After some covert searching, contacting breeders and chasing dead ends, not wanting to get the children's hopes up and not having quite got the green light from my sensible husband, one Sunday afternoon I suddenly came across 'my dog', and put myself in a place of no return. The planets aligned. He was the runt of the litter, his dad was especially small - meaning he would likely be a smaller than average dog - he had long very fluffy hair, his black and white markings weren't quite symmetrical. He has a light and dark side; his white collar not quite going all the way round his neck. On his light side, his whiskers are white, on the dark side they are black. To my mind, he was perfect. He was also unexpectedly available - having been promised to someone else who had changed their mind. Thanks to lockdown we had our first meeting via Zoom, which I first did in secret in the front cabin one evening whilst the children were watching Poirot, spinning a small white lie by telling them I was talking to a friend and not to disturb me. Needless to say I was smitten. A lengthy application form was completed and accepted by his breeder, and I broke the news to the children: 'Well.....I've found a puppy...' whereupon Celeste burst into happy tears. The only slight practical disadvantage; he was in Dudley (my middle name) on the other side of Birmingham, some five hours drive away. And this was lockdown, so we wouldn't be allowed to stay overnight in a Travelodge. The only way to collect Moses, when he was 12 weeks old and had had his second jab, would be to do the drive there and back in one hit.

I woke before my alarm went off, at about 4.30am on Saturday morning. I wasn't sure if I'd actually had any sleep, thinking about the long drive ahead and the excitement of bringing Moses home. It was our week of snow - and we had been snowed in by drifts until a couple of days before, and the roads were still covered. It was February, so it was dark. Celeste was awake early too, and we pulled on our clothes and set off into the cold pre-dawn. Celeste would be my co-pilot and the boys would stay home with Chester and await our return with the new family member.

The dawn broke as we neared Bury St Edmunds, and drove on and on to the West, passing Kettering where Thomas began his Leicester University years and spaghetti junction - which excited Celeste. As when we left London on Golden Mean twelve years previously, we were blessed with a clear bright day. Sometimes I think the weather controller knows when something momentous is happening and puts on an especially good show. We'd had a lot of snow in the East, to the point that friends were advising me to hold off a few more days. But it simply vanished the further West we drove. Celeste kept in touch with the mother ship with regular updates and recorded her own vlog of the great event. Her triple chicken sandwich and Latte were consumed before 7.30am, which felt to her like lunch time. I've never driven ten hours in one day before and am not likely to again, except in an emergency. But we had serious momentum that day.

With only the shortest of comfort breaks, we fairly glided across the country and reached Moses' birthplace by 10.30am when the rest of the world was just coming to on an uneventful Saturday morning. Then came a hardly bearable wait outside the breeder's house for a long fifteen minutes, whilst she got everything ready. Finally, the moment we had been waiting for two long weeks - or was it 20 years? - meeting Moses for the first time. Not to mention his mother Ruby and his five siblings, one of which weed all over my handbag. Moses was the shyest puppy but very happy to be cuddled, and still is. As the last and smallest pup, he'd been given extra attention and cuddles and it shows in his affectionate personality. With the form filling completed fairly quickly, Suzie his breeder bid a fond farewell and we were off again in the red van - winging our way East this time with the sun behind us, the wind in our sails and a smile on our faces. I had to do without my co-pilot on the return journey as she was happily snuggled in the back with her pup, who curled up beside her all the way home. Life with Moses had begun.

Chapter 9: Seasons

As those who spend time in Norfolk will discover its undulations, the longer we journey through our own lives the pattern of ups and downs becomes familiar. As a friend recently put it: we travel through different seasons. If we tune in to these metaphorical seasons, we can journey in greater harmony with them. Like knowing when it's time to stop titivating an oil painting, learning to recognise when a particular season has reached a natural end, and letting it go, can be cathartic. Change is a reliable constant of life, although we tend to resist it and struggle to appreciate the present of each moment. Eternal Summer might sound attractive, but wouldn't we miss the cold quiet stillness of Winter and the joy and energy that Spring brings by way of contrast? Change happens for a reason – both in nature and in our lives. To quote Julie Andrews in 'The Sound of Music'; "When one door closes, another opens....".

When asked if he'd lived in Norfolk all his life, the wise old boy's reply: "Not yet." Digby and Celeste have lived on Golden Mean all their lives – so far. No doubt they will enjoy the novelty of 'land lubbering' [if such a verb doesn't exist, it should] in the coming years, and all too soon our home educating season will come to an end. New seasons for them and for us.

Each day can be a season all by itself. Bedtime prayers offer gratitude for what was good, petition for friends who are struggling and hope for divine intervention in all that is to come. A new dawn brings new light, new hope and new challenges. Personally I'm attracted to the idea of a daily fresh start and the opportunity to do better.

We live by faith and try to trust in God's providence in our lives, cultivating an 'attitude of gratitude'. The migrating geese and swallows and the oystercatchers send heavenly signs that we are not in this alone. Our friends and neighbours are a constant blessing as we share the undulations of our lives. Living on a boat makes sharing the land that you don't own and the small space that you do a little easier; each one of us treasuring our own floating sanctuary within the wider communal space that we are fortunate enough to have on our doorstep. In the words of a song I used to sing at primary school; "When I needed a neighbour were you there, were you there?" Yes, you were.

There is something about living on a boat that fosters a spirit of adventure. The mere potential to move one's home, whether near or far, is liberating. Whilst the inner rooms of Golden Mean are indeed my sanctuary, she can provide that just as well on the Thames as on the River Waveney. She could take us to Blakeney to visit the seals or through the Caledonian Canal to visit the Lochness Monster. We recently spent an inspiring week on retreat in the Scottish Highlands and, being resistant to leave such a spiritually enriching haven, I comforted myself with pipe dreams of a mooring on nearby Loch Awe whilst the children spent their gap year giving 'A Year for God' at Craig Lodge. Travelling through the French canals to the Mediterranean is not beyond Golden Mean's capabilities, she is fit for the sea if her crew were of such a mind to do so.

Our Golden Mean season has been eighteen years – so far. We could scarcely have imagined this on that hot August day in 2003 when we walked down Pontoon N for the first time. Perhaps it's better not to know how long each season will last, simply to take each day and thank God for the blessings it brings. Let tomorrow take care of itself. It has been a season of highs and lows. Sunny days and frozen fog. Triumph and disaster. Embracing new friendships and letting go of others. Thousands of days; starting afresh with the new dawn bringing new hope.

Conclusion

October 2015 was the year we had our mast taken off. We knew it was for the best, as earlier that year some rot had been found inside, meaning it was no longer safe to have up. But it still saddened us to see our beloved mast, which we had had ever since the boat was bought in 2003, being chopped up and carted away.

Fast forward to 2021. Daddy had always said at some point we would 'get another mast'. He had been investigating about getting another for quite a while, but nothing seemed to be happening..... or so we thought.

One Wednesday in May he announced that he had received an email from Lowestoft Boat Building College, saying that they would be willing to build us one! I couldn't quite believe that we would ever see our red flag blowing in the wind at the top of our magnificent mast again, but it was happening! At the time of me writing this, they haven't built it yet, but the excitement has already arrived.

I've always loved art, and I had the honour of creating the cover of this book. As I look at it, I look at the beauty of the boat, with all its sails up, in its' 'full glory' as we say. Who knows whether we will ever put all her sails up and go to sea again. But I know if we did, it would be quite a sight. I'm sad to say I don't remember moving up here. As Mummy reads us her chapters, after she writes them, I hear about all the amazing adventures that they had on Golden Mean.

Needless to say there are many adventures I do remember, and I pray there will be many more to come. I am lucky to have grown up on such an amazing boat. And even though there are many, many lovely and beautiful boats in this world, there will never be one quite like our Golden Mean.

Celeste Harrison, May 2021

Printed in Great Britain
by Amazon

66058623R00078